# Answering
# the Big Questions

**Shane Parker**

# Answering
# the Big Questions

**NOVALIS**

© 2005 Novalis, Saint Paul University, Ottawa, Canada

Cover design: Pascale Turmel
Cover image: The Crosiers, Gene Plaisted
Layout: Renée Longtin

Business Office:
Novalis
49 Front Street East, 2nd Floor
Toronto, Ontario, Canada
M5E 1B3
Phone: 1-800-387-7164
Fax: 1-877-702-7775 or (416) 363-9409

E-mail: cservice@novalis-inc.com
www.novalis.ca

Library and Archives Canada Cataloguing in Publication

Parker, Shane A. D.
　Answering the big questions / Shane Parker.

Essays first published in the Ottawa Citizen 1999–2004.
ISBN 2-89507-486-0

　1. Theology, Doctrinal–Popular works.　2. Christian life–Anglican authors.　I. Title.

BR100.P27 2005　　　　　230　　　　C2005-900384-7

Printed in Canada.

All rights reserved. No part of this publication may be reproduced, stored in a retrieval system, or transmitted in any form, or by any means, electronic, mechanical, photocopying, recording, or otherwise, without the written permission of the publisher.

We acknowledge the financial support of the Government of Canada through the Book Publishing Industry Development Program (BPIDP) for our publishing activities.

5 4 3 2 1　　08 07 06 05 04

NOVALIS

*For my sons and daughter,
Felan, Liam and Rosemary*

# Contents

Introduction ............................................................ 7
1. Who is God? ...................................................... 9
2. What is faith about? ........................................ 17
3. How is faith lived out? ................................... 40
4. Is there faith in the world around me? ........... 61
5. Why go to church? .......................................... 82
6. Does prayer make a difference? ..................... 98
7. What role does the Bible play? .................... 106
8. Is there any sense to all the confusion? ........ 112
Conclusion ......................................................... 137

# Introduction

The words that follow were written over a period of about six years. Throughout, I worked as an Anglican priest, serving in a very public way as the Dean of a Cathedral, writing about faith regularly in the newspaper, and going about my duties as pastor. In that time my personal journey was marked by poignant movements from contentment to loss and despair, to recovery, rebuilding, hope and inner peace.

The interweaving of personal searching with the questions and issues that were posed to me from the lives of other people created occasions to reflect deeply on the faith that I had committed my life to – a faith that was alternately comforting, disconcerting, available, inaccessible, inspiring, humbling, expansive and focused.

But more than being a cause for introspection, these questions called forth expression: not the proclaiming of theology to an anonymous audience that needed to hear certain things, but words that responded to things people wanted to hear about – theology that had come through and was being spoken into the crucible of human experience.

What follows in these chapters is a series of concise reflections in the form of responses to the experiences, questions, issues and situations of many people. Together, they form something like the points of a compass, where some sense of location may be found, even when the way forward is new, uncertain or utterly confusing.

As you sail forth, may the waters, currents, shorelines and cliffs of this wondrous life – replete with the stars of the heavens – become more visible to you and lead you closer to God, the source of all life.

# 1

# Who is God?

It is plausible that our brains are wired in such a way that we can project the image of a god and worship it as though it were pre-existent. We can likewise perceive evil and imbue it with personal qualities. I have no difficulty accepting that the human mind can do such things, and even less difficulty seeing how divisions and disputes in the human family ensue from rendering these projections into systematic doctrines or ideologies.

It is also true that volunteering and exercising make people feel good, because these activities release endorphins that chase away the blues and warm the spirit. Traumatic events can create significant cognitive distortions that cause people to have horrible feelings of mistrust, anxiety, depression or powerlessness. Alcohol and drugs can make people see things that aren't there, and many people suffer from mental illnesses that cause them to hear voices or feel a special sense of divinely ordained vocation.

God, however, is wholly other; God is not "caused" by our thinking or our brain's chemistry. God is experienced as peace that passes all understanding, as hope that exists when there is little cause for hope, and as love that is constant. The experience of God results in a compelling desire to live altruistically, as we discover in the Hebrew and Christian scriptures; in the traditions that stem in an unbroken line from the very first Christian communities; and in the evolution, progression and application of reason. Where scripture, tradition and reason meet personal experience, God is revealed.

It is logical that our mortal bodies and their complex systems are wired to grasp and be affected by God; it would have been a significant oversight if the Creator had not allowed the evolution of humanity to be conscious of its origins, its sustenance and its destiny. But this does not mean we are made to create God; while we can create, fight and die for any number of gods, God the Creator of all calls us to find our true nature in God's love.

## The way to God

The Christian tradition affirms that God is uniquely revealed in Jesus Christ. In other words, if you want to know what God is all about, look to Jesus and you will find the answer.

Christianity holds the belief that God, the transcendent and eternal Creator of all things, visited time and space in the person of Jesus to show for all time that God is with us and that God is love. Through Jesus, God tells all creation that nothing can be separated from God's redeeming love, and that we will find salvation – the discovery of true life – when we accept and share God's love.

God, in Jesus, shows all women, men and children that those who completely entrust their lives to God can become radically free to give sacrificially to this world – to live as spiritually strong people who, with humility and confidence, seek to serve others and to challenge anything that injures, corrupts or destroys the integrity of all that God has made to be good and just.

Christians believe that the way to God is the way of Jesus; wise Christians know that the way to God is not bound by simplistic verbal formulas and tribal or cultural affiliations. God is found in joy, peace, patience, kindness, goodness, faithfulness, gentleness and self-control; those who live by the Spirit also walk by the Spirit, and in so doing, show the way to God.

## In God's image

The philosopher Voltaire is quoted as saying, "If God made us in his own image, we have more than reciprocated." There is always a danger that people will recreate God in an image that suits their notions of how to be in the world. Some will make and worship a strong, powerful, masculine God; others, a gentle, nurturing, feminine God. But God is profoundly free to be who God is, and that may have very little to do with what people want God to be.

To say that we are made in the image of God does not refer to our male or female bodies. The image of God that is found in humanity is our positive, creative and loving nature. We are free to reflect God's nature in our lives, choosing to use our human form and faculties to live in harmony with God and all creation. We are also free to deny God or to choose a destructive path through life. Even our freedom to choose reflects the divine nature.

Saying that God has masculine and feminine attributes is completely consistent with the Christian tradition as it has been received through the ages. However, it is not acceptable to say that God is male or female. The addressing of God as Father or Mother is not a description of gender, but of the nature of God. It would be just as accurate to describe God as love, Spirit, bread, vine, shepherd, hen, or even Word.

How we address God has much to do with how God is revealed to us and how we experience our relationship with God. Nevertheless, God must be respected as entirely "other," always a bit of a mystery to us, always challenging us to deepen our relationship and to taste more fully God's love, peace, joy and hope.

## Artistic portrayals of Jesus

If I had the skills of an artist and sought to paint an accurate portrait of Jesus, I could not look to anyone's memory or to a historical record for inspiration. Nor could I draw together some kind of composite image from the work of other artists. Even the Bible is silent on this subject. In order to paint Jesus, I could rely only on what I know about him.

Portraits of Jesus are never accurate in the sense of capturing the actual image of his face. No artist can claim do have done such a portrait. But representations of Jesus do attempt to capture who he is and to invite the viewer to contemplate the truth of his divinity or the compelling mystery of his power and presence.

Christian spirituality is about faith in the person of Jesus. This faith has continued to exist because people continue to encounter him. Once they have had such an encounter, the desire to express the reality of Jesus is very strong. Some people write poetry or music, others simply speak of what they have experienced, and still others try to bring the contours of his presence to visual art. Such is the vivid beauty of the encounter. Christ, who touches human hearts with transforming love, must be expressed and shared through human sounds, sights and senses.

For this reason, representational art, no less than music or words, has a very important place in the Christian tradition, and is something to be encouraged and celebrated. Art that attempts to represent the image of Jesus often seeks to express the experience of faith in the person of Jesus, and therefore serves as a tangible witness of his presence.

## The wrath of God

Ascribing human attributes to God is a risky business. At the same time, Christians believe that God is revealed in the person Jesus, who was fully human and therefore had a full range of emotions. Jesus demonstrated anger when he chased out of a place of prayer several unscrupulous people who were profiting from the vulnerability of others. He also rebuked his closest follower, Peter, who tried to prevent Jesus from giving his life out of love.

We read in the book of Exodus in the Bible that the wrath of God was kindled against Moses when, despite all kinds of reassurances, Moses was unwilling to return to Egypt and bring release to a captive people. At several points in the journey of Moses and his people through the wilderness, God's anger was manifest in the form of rebuke and punishment.

It is fair to say that God gets angry and punishes people. It is not fair to say that God does so with reckless or random impunity. Christians believe that God has been revealed as love, and that the movement of God's Spirit enables God's love to be known in human hearts and shown in human lives.

Hearts can be hardened or broken by the rollercoaster ride of life, and people can become estranged from God's love, or insecure within themselves. Such estrangement and insecurity can cause people, at times unwillingly, to do destructive things to others or to themselves. I believe that this is contrary to the will of God, and that God freely acts in whatever way is best to melt or heal people's hearts. This may include something that feels like anger or punishment, but the purpose is always to call forth a deep and robust love in the heart of every human being.

## Final judgment

The ancient Christian creeds speak of God in Jesus as one who "will come again to judge the living and the dead." While this appears to suggest that all of humanity will be judged at the end of time, in a so-called final judgment, we also believe that our lives are under the scrutiny of God's judgment even now.

For some, the notion of God as one to whom all hearts are open and all desires known, and from whom no secrets are hidden, appears to be an invasive, neuroses-inducing idea – possibly even immobilizing, as though one wrong move will result in condemnation. For others, the idea of facing God after death for a final tallying is like hoping for the best after submitting a final exam you may or may not have been prepared for. Instead, the judgment of God in our lives is an active, enabling force, because it is about God finding ways to liberate us rather than squash us. Jesus said, "I have come to give you life in abundance," and consistently points to himself as the way to everlasting life.

The judgment of God in Christ enables us to see ourselves as God sees us, sorting and sifting the thoughts and intentions of our hearts, and correcting us when we are in spiritual peril. The parables of Jesus repeatedly point to the urgency of following God's will: the separation of sheep and goats, the judgment of those who love God and others and those who do not, is never held up as a distant event that matters little to the present. Obedience to God matters now, and we are called – and enabled – to conduct ourselves accordingly.

# 2

# What is faith about?

To say you "have a lot of faith" in a friend, spouse or co-worker suggests trust, predictability, affection, respect – maybe even reliance or dependence. Faith assumes you have a relationship with the person or thing you have faith in. Faith in God is no different. Religious faith stems from being in some kind of relationship with God, both in terms of coming to an understanding of who God is revealed to be in the Bible, and in the way you experience God in your own life.

Faith is a relationship with God that encompasses feelings that extend far beyond sentiments of trust, affection or dependence. Faith in God finds expression in the full range of emotions, including anger, blame, frustration, loss, sadness, fear, unbelief, comfort, strength, calm, love, peace or joy. Faith in God is about discerning God's presence in the many movements and moments that give shape to your journey – from the most difficult and vexing to the most pleasant and satisfying. Ultimately, faith speaks of the divine companionship that is with you and fully part of the whole story of your life.

## Does faith make a difference?

Although I have always had some kind of belief in God and have always been connected to the Anglican Church, there have been significant times in my life when I honestly could not see that my faith made any difference at all. Twice in my life, once as a boy of twelve and once as a man of forty-one, tragedy changed my course forever, replacing my sense of belonging and well-being with disturbing feelings of being abandoned. Invariably, these were times when, for any number of reasons, I was not conscious of the presence of God. Life seemed devoid of meaning, as though all was transient and fickle, easily crumbled by the consequences of human choices and the limits of human finitude.

What always draws me back from these moments is the quiet conviction that in the midst of life are a strength and constancy that are independent of people, situations, places or things. No amount of sophisticated questioning or nasty situations has been able to diminish this conviction for me.

I find it very easy to express my faith in the language of the Christian tradition. I believe that we can look to the life, death and resurrection of Jesus and understand that God is with us, visiting us with the Holy Spirit, and offering to us endless possibilities, especially when there appear to be no possibilities at all. To grasp the meaning of this, even tentatively, is to receive a sense of hope that is both alluring and enabling.

It is perfectly reasonable to say "Why bother?" if faith in God does not provide meaning and purpose to your life. If you can see why faith matters, then it is equally reasonable to do all you can to strengthen and celebrate your faith, especially within a solid, rational worshipping community.

Worship reminds me of the beauty of God in the midst of life. I feel renewed as I taste the presence of God in the elements of worship – in hearing and seeing and speaking and singing timeless words and symbols. God is often present to people in worship as peace that cannot be explained by logic or reason. Such peace stills and comforts world-weary souls, and leads us forward in a gentle, mighty breath of new meaning and purpose.

### How can any modern person believe in God?

Theology, as a discipline, begins with an experience of the divine, an encounter with the Creator of Creation. Fundamentally, theology attempts to assign words to such an encounter. When the words of theology become too far removed from the experience of the divine, then they simply become part of a body of knowledge that can be studied dispassionately and accepted or dismissed as reasonable, logical or plausible.

A simple syllogism can summarize my basic theology. In Jesus, God is revealed as love; we are made in the image of God; we find our true nature when we receive and give God's love. No magic formulas, no spells or potions. By following the way of Jesus we find the deepest and richest experience of God, and we find ourselves.

I remain a Christian because I once encountered the divine in a moment of being unexpectedly visited by an experience of peace that coursed through me in a moment: literally crying out in utter despair only to be immediately and profoundly reassured. This experience strengthened me and gave me a reason to live in hope, certain that my life and all life were held by a love that changes lives. I gather regularly with others to revisit that experience in story, songs and symbols, and to receive, actually and physically, a taste of the love of God in Christ in the form of bread and wine.

In the Cathedral where I serve is found one of my favourite symbols of God: way up high in the clerestory is a stone carving of a mother pelican feeding her young with her own flesh and blood. While this may not be an accurate scientific depiction, it is, I believe, an accurate theological statement. When we are fully alive in the love of God and fully strengthened in spirit, we can give to the world in a way that is like the truth and stark beauty revealed in that carving.

## Discovering God

If the truth of God's existence could be known only after we die, then faith in God during our mortal lives would always be conditional or tentative, never completely certain. If God could not be discovered before we die, we would not be able to know God's love or be affected by God's challenge to love others as we know ourselves to be loved. It is doubtful whether the idea of God would have any foothold in our world if there were not some way of discovering the divine in human history.

I believe that we speak of God, or seek God, or even deny God, because God has chosen to be present to people throughout the course of time. Countless human lives have been deeply affected by their encounter with a profound, creative goodness that is wholly outside of themselves and is commonly called "God." Religious experience of this order is almost always characterized by acts of faithful affirmations of God, hand in hand with altruistic love towards other people.

In the Christian tradition, it is not possible to state that the truth of God will be discovered only in the afterlife. Christians believe that the eternal love of God has been fully revealed in Jesus, and that through the abiding presence of the Holy Spirit in creation, people are brought into communion with God in Jesus. This means that God's friendship was clearly shown to us by Jesus, who walked with ordinary people, healed them, ate and drank with the least loved, challenged the most loved, and felt the worst things of life. Jesus shows us that God is faithful and present before, during and after death, offering us hope that enables and love that compels.

Christians believe that prayer to God, the genuine seeking of God's presence, will be answered, and that the Spirit of God will enter into the lives of all who seek truth. Christians also believe that God freely chooses to surprise people, and that to expect the unexpected is a good way to notice the movement of the Spirit. God can be discovered now, and lives are positively changed by such a wonderful, marvellous thing.

## Why Jesus died

While we can speculate on hypothetical scenarios concerning the death of Jesus, the compelling reality is that he did not die of old age. As one of my former professors would say, "Jesus didn't die of a heart attack; he was killed because of what he said about God." Jesus was not killed because he spoke about love and forgiveness, or because he healed people. He was killed because he identified himself with God.

The killing of Jesus could have ended everything and left him forgotten, confined to the past, but it did not because God raised him from the dead. This gave history reason to notice Jesus of Nazareth. After encountering the Risen Christ, the apostles did not go about simply teaching the golden rule or telling anecdotes of Jesus duelling with religious authorities. Instead, they went about proclaiming Jesus as Lord, the Son of God, whom God had raised from the dead.

I have often heard people say that God is relatively easy to accept, but Jesus presents a difficulty. Perhaps this is because Jesus poses a clear question: if he is not what God is all about, then what do you think God is all about?

Christians believe that God is revealed in Jesus. In the life and death of Jesus, God shows that God abides with us always, even in the worst things. Through the resurrection and risen life of Jesus, God shows that new life and new hope are God's response to all that would destroy life and hope. Jesus reveals the Creator of Creation to us in passionate, loving terms, and asks us to accept that in him we see the true nature of God.

## The Resurrection

On Easter Day it is customary for Christians to greet one another by saying, "Christ is Risen!" When someone greets me in this way, I feel that I am in the company of a witness to the resurrection. My faith is stirred when I hear the voice of faith in another.

A seventeenth-century Dutch carol puts it this way: "Had Christ, that once was slain, ne'er burst his three-day prison, our faith had been in vain: but now hath Christ arisen!" Christianity would not exist if the resurrection of Jesus had not occurred.

Christian faith was born at Easter. The persistent proclamation that Jesus had been raised from the dead caused history to pause and note his life – there was no other reason for him to be remembered, worshipped or interpreted by subsequent generations. If something truly extraordinary had not happened to Jesus after his death, he probably would soon have been forgotten.

Something extraordinary did happen, something that was clearly observed by Jesus' contemporaries. On the third day after he died on a cross and was buried in a tomb, he appeared again, alive and recognizable. Women and men saw him and knew him, and they spoke of what they saw to others.

This is a key point when considering whether the resurrection of Jesus was an objective historical event: those who knew him before his death recognized him after his resurrection. The Risen Christ was able to re-establish his relationships with the people he was closest to in life. In this sense, the resurrection can be historically "proven": it happened in relation to real people who spoke of their encounters with the resurrected Jesus in lucid, concrete terms.

Christian faith is Easter faith. The resurrection of Jesus revealed the truth of who he was, and made his life and death rich with meaning. The spirit of the Risen Christ enabled the strong faith of the early Church and has ensured the faith of every generation since. The resurrection confirmed that God had revealed God's very nature to the world through Jesus – and so established the core belief of Christianity: we look to Jesus and find God.

At Easter, Christians celebrate the wonderful mystery of God casting aside the boundaries of time and space, and the limits of our understanding, causing us to see the powerful love that fills creation with meaning, purpose and hope. To this we respond, "He is risen indeed, Alleluia!"

## Suffering and healing

Life on this earth is fragile and fleeting, a precious thing, easily broken by circumstances, choices and consequences. Creation is utterly free, and replete with all the elements of freedom, including natural or human-made disasters. No one is immune from either the delights or the dangers of this world, and so much of what we look to for reassurance can fall away as quickly as life itself. When it does, we feel our faith is being tested, and questions like "Why is God doing this?" quickly spring to mind.

The Christian belief that God is present in suffering is quite different from the notion that God is simply on the outside of life, watching impotently, or choosing in a fickle way to help some and ignore others.

Christian faith nurtures a sense of hope and trust that is steadfast even in the worst disasters. The suffering of Jesus on the cross is a sign that God is no stranger to human suffering, and freely chooses to identify with both the joys and traumas of mortal life. The resurrection of Jesus is the definitive sign of

God's power over Creation: nothing, not even death, is stronger than God, and no despair is greater than hope.

Sometimes people look for God to save them from suffering – as though they could literally be pulled out of harm's way – and are often left wondering why they are not rescued.

Others come to feel the compassionate presence of God with them in suffering and receive a profound gift of healing in the form of inner calm – a peace that passes all understanding.

Christian hope declares that God is constant, and that God's love reaches into time and space and touches our deepest needs for meaning when suffering, disaster or disease threatens to overwhelm and conquer our spirits. To recognize that God is not distant from our suffering can be life-changing.

## What is sin?

Sin, natural urges and breaking the law are three different things. To sin is to disobey the commandments of God, by action or inaction, in thought, word or deed. Following a natural urge can range from falling in love to committing murder. Breaking the law can involve everything from jaywalking to genocide. Following urges or breaking the law may or may not be a sin.

Christians believe that sin prevents us from growing into the full stature of Christ, and affects the unity of the church community; Christians also believe that true repentance results in the forgiveness of sins by God and allows for a brand-new beginning for the sinner and restoration to full participation in the life of the Church.

In other words, when someone sins, or misses the mark, all is not lost. The Holy Spirit enables us to see our sinfulness and to become contrite, desiring to make amends. For a person of faith, sin injures the spirit and distracts from feelings of well-being or wholeness. Forgiveness is therefore healing and restorative. Anyone who has "come clean" after sinning knows the tremendous feeling of relief that flows from such honesty.

Before a midwinter's night snowfall, there is a mess of footprints, soiled snow banks, and crusty, broken surfaces. New snow layers over the old, affected by existing contours but taking on an entirely new surface upon which an utterly new day begins. "Belief" in sin is inextricably linked to forgiveness of sin and the possibility of new life.

## Are some sins worse than others?

The Anglican tradition has tended to approach the idea of sin as affecting one's relationship with God and feelings of well-being. For this reason, not much attention has been given to weighting or categorizing sins. It matters that people become alienated from God; how this comes to be – whether by indifferent, irreligious, immoral or illegal behaviour – is important only insofar as people feel burdened, tormented or isolated.

Holding before people who are distressed by their sins the possibility of God's forgiveness enables them to unburden themselves from the disabling feelings associated with sin, and restores them to an enabling relationship with God — which in turn allows them to face their responsibilities to others.

## Revenge and forgiveness

Statements like "love your enemies," "do good to those who harm you," or "turn the other cheek" make it quite clear that revenge has no place in the vocabulary of Christian spirituality. Forgiveness is the response Christians are to strive for in their dealings with others.

The life of Jesus is inaugurated by John the Baptist, who administered a baptism of repentance for the forgiveness of sins. In the teaching of Jesus, forgiveness is central, both as a gift from God that is virtually unlimited and as a defining feature of God's kingdom. Even the crucifixion of Jesus displays divine forgiveness: when Jesus forgives his executioners, and in the ultimate act of repentance and forgiveness his death represents.

Christian teaching underlines forgiveness both as something extended from God to people, and as something people are to extend to one another. Divine love and human love are to be connected by forgiveness: the Lord's Prayer says, "forgive us our sins as we forgive those who sin against us." Jesus' parable of the unmerciful debtor gives a grim illustration of the parallel between forgiveness from God and the imperative to forgive others: one who was forgiven a debt fails to extend the same forgiveness to another indebted to him, and is, consequently, severely punished. This parable also illustrates the point that vengeance is indeed the domain of the Lord.

To extend forgiveness as God forgives is not possible without God's help. When someone has been hurt or betrayed, withholding forgiveness is a normal first response. Those who are physically, emotionally or spiritually disenfranchised can hardly be commanded to "turn the other cheek." The grace to forgive is a gift from God, which flows from inner peace and serenity of spirit. The ability to forgive is a sign that God has been allowed into a person's life, and has given that person the tremendous strength it takes to show mercy to those who would normally be subjected to revenge.

## What is the soul?

A soul is not something we have. Our soul – our spirit – is who God has made us to be: our souls are who we are. To speak of a person's life, or to say that someone is a kindly soul or has a fighting spirit, suggests that our identities are not completely described by our physical bodies, although our bodies are intrinsic to our earthly existence. Physical bodies enable us to be present on this earth, to touch, taste, hear or see, and to acknowledge the presence of others. This also means that our bodies, like the earth, have a fragility to them, and can be much affected by what happens around us or inside of us.

After our life on earth has ended and our vulnerable bodies cease to be, we assume spiritual lives. Each person is thus distinctly defined, continuously and uniquely, forever, whether on earth or in eternity. The fifteenth chapter of the First Letter of Paul to the Corinthians develops this belief more fully.

An ancient creed of the Church states that God is "the maker of heaven and earth, of all that is seen and unseen." This means that the universe is good, the work of a single, loving Creator. This also means that all souls are of God and are therefore worthy of care, respect and safety. It follows that any who would seek to undermine the well-being of others must be withstood, preferably (but, sadly, not always) without the use of violence.

During the rite of Christian baptism we commit our souls to God and, among other things, promise to "strive for justice and peace among all people" and to "respect the dignity of every human being." If God has created all life, then life and every living being is imbued with meaning and purpose. One finds true meaning and purpose when the Creator's purpose for creation is discovered: that there be peace on earth and goodwill towards all.

## Do animals have souls?

The question of animals "having" souls presumably is not about whether animals are embodied spirits, but whether they are uniquely created beings with identities that "pass on" after death, as people are. Although this question often arises when someone has lost a beloved animal companion, it is not answered in a specific or definitive manner in the Christian tradition. Christians believe that God is the creator of "heaven and earth," of all that is "seen and unseen."

It is not difficult to believe that if all forms of life on earth have been created by a loving God, they are somehow imbued with purpose, and will somehow return to God when their time on earth has passed. In other words, lives that have been made by God are God's, and will find that their destiny is in God, be they pesky blackflies, loveable puppies or human beings. All created beings, whether souls or not, exist in this marvellous hope.

## Can a person be possessed?

The phenomenon of possession and the ministry of deliverance still have currency in the Christian tradition. In the Anglican Church, if it appears as though someone is afflicted, the bishop must be informed, and no fewer than two priests must work in consultation with the bishop and mental health professionals to determine the best course of action.

We live in a society that has an odd preoccupation with things paranormal. Some people of faith appear to have a satanology that is more developed and absorbing than orthodox theology. Language and symbols are powerful tools that try to explain what people experience, but we must always try to withstand the temptation to give undue emphasis to things that are injurious to the fragile emotional or spiritual health of others.

Christians believe that God in Christ is Lord of all, and that evil is not a force equal to the Creator of Creation. Giving undeserved credibility to anything that corrupts and destroys the creatures of God must be firmly renounced by people of faith. Belief in God should not be spurred by an exaggerated belief in some kind of opposing force; God is intrinsically good and so is all that God has made.

It is human nature to choose badly, and we are finite beings who are prone to any number of afflictions. The language and symbols of healing and reconciliation are better things with which to preoccupy our minds.

## What is hell?

I sometimes wonder whether people seek verification or refutation when asking about the existence of hell. In either case, it is probably wiser in the long run to dwell on heavenly things.

In the Bible, "hell" is described using a wide range of colourful and often very disturbing images. For some reason, fire is a popular biblical image, although Dante depicts the lowest level of hell as an icy horror, where souls are forever sealed, cut off from everything. Some theologians argue that hell is simply non-being, the quenching of otherwise everlasting life. I believe hell is an undesirable fate, like living without God's friendship, rather than a place.

Although images are not literal depictions, and arguments are imprecise, the idea of hell says something about divine judgment, which cannot be dismissed. Most allusions to the afterlife describe how our immortal souls are subject to God's righteous scrutiny, and how the ultimate destiny of those who accept God's will is decidedly different from those who do not. This means God is somehow aware of the myriad choices people freely make, and that some choices imperil our spiritual well-being. This also means God is profoundly moral, and, in the end, does not allow evil to go unchecked.

In the Christian tradition, it is not possible to speak of divine judgment without considering the inexorable pull of God's redemptive love, perfectly revealed in Jesus. Christianity also affirms that nothing, not even death, can separate us from this redeeming love.

We should be very reluctant, then, to accept anything that suggests that God's judgment or redemption is limited to our actions or omissions during the short span of our lives on earth. Moreover, it is highly likely that each of us, either in this life or beyond, will be confronted by God's powerful and demanding love. It is highly unlikely that anyone will turn away, unrepentant and unaffected.

Occasionally, it may be necessary to describe what is meant by hell. However, it would be perverse to use the idea of hell as an incentive for someone to believe in God. The incentive to unite our lives to God, to accept grace, mercy, justice and peace for ourselves and for all creation, lies in God, who is love.

## Getting into heaven

Even though winning gold stars in the personal behaviour department is good, that alone is not what gets someone into heaven. There is a lot of room in God's imagination for the rest of us – including those who may not have an expressed belief in God (although we might wonder why anyone who doesn't believe in God would worry about getting into heaven). I worship regularly with people who, like me, have at times behaved badly or made poor choices. It is good to be forgiven and restored with like-minded people, and it will be good to greet them in heaven.

Different religions (and their respective denominations or strands) have different ways of expressing or dictating "God's standards for personal behaviour." On one end of the spectrum, some believe that stringent standards govern all aspects of human behaviour; on the other end of the spectrum, some believe that God sets non-prescriptive, relativistic standards for being in the world. A person looking for a way of living that will ensure entry into heaven could spend a lot of time studying which standards of behaviour might work best.

Jesus teaches that we are close to the kingdom of God when we realize that our lives are held in the beauty and power of God's love and become free to share that love with others. The Hebrew prophet Micah says that we are required "to do justice, and to love kindness, and to walk humbly with your God." Loving God (and being loved by God) and seeking to love others as we would love ourselves is the golden rule for most world religions – probably because life is much, much easier when we adopt this standard of behaviour.

Human beings are made in the image of God, and we find our true selves when we behave in ways that are creative, altruistic, nurturing, forgiving and hopeful. We get a taste of heaven when God's love is borne out in human communities, which is God's passionate desire for every child, woman and man – and ours to reject or receive.

## Miracles

Miracles do happen and can be expected, but we cannot set up the conditions for a miracle on our own.

Christians understand miracles to be events that are so obviously beyond natural causes that they can only be attributed to divine intervention. In other words, God directly changes the normal course of things to produce an outcome that would not otherwise occur. Miracles are acts of God that are so distinctive, those who experience or witness them become aware of a power that passes understanding, and suggests that the waters of history flow within the boundless ocean of God.

Most of the "miracles" attributed to Jesus are more accurately referred to as "power" or "signs." The power of God is shown through the wonders of Jesus as signs of God's presence in him and, subsequently, in his true followers. The power shown through Jesus invariably demonstrated a goodness that only extended outward and took nothing in return. The power of God in Jesus is seen as a perfect, complete and entirely benevolent gift that reveals the nature of God.

Miracles can occur as God freely chooses to act within creation to show forth powerful love and to draw attention to the possibility that there is always more than we can see or know about the unfolding of life. The subtext of the Christian gospel is to expect the unexpected, and to trust that the unfettered benevolence of God will prevail. The best miracles are the ones that transform hardened hearts and grim faces into things of warmth and peace.

## Faith and science

In an Anglican Eucharistic Prayer, we give thanks to God for creating a universe replete with "stars, galaxies and planets," and for bringing forth the human race from "primal elements," blessing us with "memory, reason and skill." This prayer obviously acknowledges the insights of science, and uses the lens of science to recognize God as the author of an intricate, lengthy and magnificent process of creation, where sophisticated human life evolved in the context of a sweeping wave of divine artistry.

The *Book of Common Prayer* contains a prayer that reads, "O God, whose Spirit filleth all the world, revealing the wonders of nature through each succeeding day: we thank thee for the continual advance in medical science." Clearly, scientific progress can be desirable and we thank God when human memory, reason and skill are used to good purpose.

Science can help the world to be a better place, but science can also be used to create effective weapons of mass destruction and products or processes that are detrimental to the environment. Science can also – sometimes inadvertently, sometimes not – set the conditions and means for us to modify the basic structures of life in ways that are ethically dubious. To suggest that science is always and only a blessing is to turn a blind eye to the propensity for science to interfere with peace and harmony on earth.

Science is not always a blessing, but neither is it always a curse. When science clearly serves the common good and stretches us to conceive of new ways of alleviating illness and hunger, or to provide useful tools or constructive toys, then there is every reason to give thanks. When scientists develop knowledge that works against the common good and well-being of all people, then there is every reason to sound the alarm. Scientists, like the rest of us, are free to do good or evil, and we are all free, as our conscience guides us, to enjoy, ignore, challenge or judge the fruits of scientific inquiry.

## The cruel food chain?

I love to watch hawks circling in the sky, keen eyes on the lookout. I once saw a kestrel grab a sparrow in mid-air, quickly dispatching it with strong talons. Another time I saw a young bear rooting under an old log, scooping up grubs (and anything else that appeared to move). A spider's web is an amazing thing to encounter on a dewy morning, glistening as it awaits the arrival of an unsuspecting fly. And the incredible movements of bats as they dip and turn to catch mosquitoes is a marvel of flight.

One winter after a light dusting of snow, I walked along the Carp Ridge, and saw evidence of a fox pursuing a rabbit, and the perfect outline of an owl's wings on either side of a tiny patch of blood where a mouse's tracks abruptly stopped. High above in a tree, two porcupines sat gnawing away at the upper branches of a large oak tree, stripping it bare (and leaving an enormous mound of droppings at the base of the tree in the process).

On a farm in Luskville, I took part in the slaughtering of cows, learning how to skin and butcher the carcasses, watching life become food; it was a poignant moment in understanding the import of giving thanks before eating. Whether harvesting food from living plants or living animals, the reliance of human beings on other forms of life for food is well worth thinking about.

I believe that the diversity of species and the fine balance that is effected by predator and prey are a wondrous part of God's creation. The humane raising and slaughtering of livestock or hunting and fishing for food is not cruel, but upsetting the ecological balance and the destruction of species by pollution, habitat destruction or over-consumption is very wrong.

The instinctive predator is integral to creation, but the willful misuse of creation by human beings is a function of our desire to have more and of our disregard for the interconnectedness of life on earth. Instead of asking whether the food chain is cruel, it may be more apt to ask why we, who are made in God's image, don't fervently seek to bring all our wisdom and skill to ensuring that we do not further degrade the marvellous and intricate world we share with all of God's creatures.

# 3

# How is faith lived out?

One of the most penetrating questions a faithful person can be asked is "How does your faith affect the way you live?" The good news is that faith is meant to be lived out in daily life, rather than in some kind of separate, protected, holy realm. Christian faith is never intended to be a personal, private matter, sheltered from the mundane or maddening stuff of life.

Sometimes faith provides clear guidance; sometimes faith will cause you to pause and reflect more deeply; sometimes faith will be silent as waves of complexity rise around you. Just as Jesus ate and drank with outcasts and sinners and encountered the best and worst of things – even while journeying with decidedly human friends – a life of faith will bring you, as a person of faith, into all of the situations and issues that can possibly arise in the great ocean of time and space.

## Faith and daily life

Christians believe that God is revealed to them in the person of Jesus and is present to them in the Holy Spirit. We look to Jesus and we see God revealed as love – a love that we are called to seek and to emulate, enabling us to taste and to share the fullness of what God wills for every human being.

In his first letter to the Church in Corinth, St. Paul describes divine love as patient and empowering, not anxious to impress or boast; neither is it possessive or controlling. This love is considerate, unselfish and forgiving; does not keep accounts of the shortcomings of others; and is glad when goodness and truth prevail.

Daily life demands some kind of response from us. It is impossible to be unaffected by the good, bad and indifferent things that happen to you and everybody else all over the world every moment of the day. You can respond in kind to what is placed before you, or you can choose to look deeply into the heart of Christianity and respond with generosity of spirit and self-control.

You often will be imperfect in your response, and the results may not be what you wish for, but Christians believe that the Spirit instructs and comforts those who seek the truth. As you give love, so will love abide in you, and you will come to see how you are loved by God – and that will help you move through daily life more serenely than words can say.

## Saints today

I am concerned when I hear statements that appear to present our society in largely negative terms. While we can easily point to troubling situations and destructive behaviours, we must also affirm that which is good and life-giving. If we convince ourselves that everything is rather hopeless, we encourage despair and apathy. If we are convinced that every situation can benefit from human kindness and creativity, then we encourage hope and action.

Biblical characters are often seen as being distant, different and altogether more saintly than we are. This is unfortunate. I suspect that many of them were normal, reluctant souls who were simply led to faith and action by the combination of God's powerful call and the reality of their society's needs. Ordinary people shine brightly when moved by the Holy Spirit to engage the situations they face.

This is equally true today. God changes people's lives. A person's eyes can be opened to what God's love and justice are all about, and be drawn into very new ways of being and acting. For this reason, I believe saints and prophets are always nearby. Perhaps they are not that obvious to a culture that loves large heroes and grand gestures, but there are always people who remind us of what is truly good, and who encourage us to do the same.

Mother Teresa was undoubtedly an exceptional woman in whom the countenance of Christ was evident. It is interesting to note that she chose to minister in the very heart of human misery, to people cast aside by others. Ironically, sick and troubled parts of society, by their very nature, encourage saintly activity. Those who are called to love as God loves are drawn to act where God loves to make God's presence known. That is the rule, rather than the exception.

## Faith and healing

Some people cling to a hope of being able to conquer illness right up to the moment of death. Other people lose hope at the first sign of illness and are pleasantly surprised when things are miraculously or medically brought under control. Perhaps those who are enabled to face life with hope, and illness without fear, have received the gift that God would give to each of us. Looking to religion to conquer illness, however, may place unrealistic expectations on those who are unwell or on those who minister to them.

I would say that our faith or spirituality is important in how we cope with illness. If religion is something that nurtures a sense of hope and trust, then it can provide an important frame of reference when we are unwell. Being able to find meaning in suffering, or simply to know that God is not distant from our pain, can be life-changing.

The Christian belief that God is present in suffering is quite different from the notion that God is simply on the outside of human pain waiting to "cure" people, like pulling someone out of a big hole in the ground. Sometimes people look for God in the wrong place when illness strikes, and wonder why they are not being rescued. Others come to feel the presence of God with them in times of suffering and apparent hopelessness and receive a profound gift of healing – especially when the illness is intractable, and nasty conditions prevail until death takes them away.

Ministering to those who are unwell is of course easier when they are optimistic and brave. The reality is that each person brings their own story to illness, and when people are made vulnerable by news that they are ill, all kinds of unbidden insecurities can come into play. In the end, the faith and hope of the ministering person, and her or his ability to empathize and connect with the story of the one who is unwell, are what make ministering "easier." When people conquer their debilitating feelings of isolation from others and from God that often accompany illness, true and lasting healing begins.

## Christmas faith

Christmas can be a very stressful time of year. There are so many layers of expectations placed on the season that some people spend the weeks leading up to it feeling pressured to make everything nice, and to somehow draw together all their feelings of love and goodwill into one day with the right gift for everyone.

Christmas can be a bit tyrannical, if the truth be told, and I would invite everybody to keep things simple for themselves and others – to enjoy the day and one another and let go of anything that gets in the way of doing so.

For Christians, Christmas is but one special moment in the year-round celebration of God who comes to the whole world in great simplicity – God with us, among us, within our midst, in our hearts. Holy simplicity. True life is found in trusting God as Jesus did, and in continually seeking the guidance of the Holy Spirit, which has a lot to do with simply letting yourself be loved and strengthened so you can give love and strength to others, every day of your life.

Keep your faith by keeping it simple. Enjoy the day and savour all it means for every day of the year. Find a gentle, welcoming church that has timeless ritual and let yourself go into the glorious possibilities of the powerful, transforming love of the Creator of Creation. Gather with loved ones and strangers there on the Feast of the Birth of Christ and give thanks that God comes to us in great gentleness and simplicity.

## Faith and wealth

If financial success is a sign of God's blessing, and the lack of wealth is an indication of punishment, then I have been punished by God for my entire adult life. The truth is that there are rich and poor people who are faithful, gracious and loving, and there are rich and poor people who are not. Neither wealth nor poverty can insulate people from blessings, loss or pain. At all times and in every situation, the Creator gives in abundance to anyone who would receive grace to live life well.

Christianity will never assert that wealth is a sign of God's blessing. Jesus taught that the poor are blessed, and that it is easier for a large, laden camel to pass through a tiny portal than it is for someone whose first priority is wealth and possessions to grasp what God is all about. He taught that where our heart is, there will our treasure be also.

If wealth is what you seek, you may or may not achieve your goal; in any event, your quest matters little in the grand scheme of things. If you are financially successful (or talented in whatever way) and you use your life to glorify God by serving others with generosity of spirit, you are close to the will of God and you are blessed.

## Dressing for success

St. Paul offers advice on a full range of clothing and accessories. As a start, and to establish a fresh, positive foundation, he strongly advises discarding our old nature and its deeds, and putting on the new nature of Christ, which features constant renewal in the image of the Creator.

For everyday wear, he recommends garments of compassion, kindness, humility, gentleness, patience, forbearance, forgiveness and love. When heading out for a difficult day, he advocates a belt of truth, a coat of integrity, shoes of peace, a shield of faith, the helmet of salvation and the sword of God's word.

There are no prescribed "visual identifiers" in the Christian tradition. Although many people wear the image of a cross, Christians are to be identified by their manner of living rather than their manner of dress. It is the inner person and what flows from the heart that matter.

## Ups and downs

In the Second Book of Samuel, the prophet Nathan tells King David a parable of two men, one rich and one poor. The rich man, who had herds of livestock, took from the poor man his only lamb to feed a guest. Nathan asks David what he thought of this. David is indignant, and says the rich man's actions were reprehensible and he deserves to die. Nathan then says to David, "You are the man!" David suddenly sees himself in the parable and is devastated by his own insensitivity as a wealthy king. His life is changed dramatically by this new self-awareness.

The use of stories to enable people to examine their lives is common in sacred scripture. When we identify with a character in the story, a new perspective is possible. With new perspective comes the chance to choose a new way of being in the world, a way that is closer to the will of God, and less fraught with the distractions that take us away from finding spiritual peace.

The fortunes and misfortunes of the high-tech world, for example, bring to mind the parable of two builders, one who built a house on rock and another who built a house on sand. When the rain fell, the floods came and the winds blew, the house founded on rock did not fall, but the one built on sand fell, "and great was its fall." Jesus likened those who hear and act on what he taught to the one who built on rock, and those who hear and do not act to the one who built on sand.

The basic lesson that can be learned from the roller-coaster high-tech market is that we should not place too much of our sense of security on anything mortal. Markets can collapse, people can die, relationships can end, computers can break down and plumbing can leak. We can give our mind and heart to markets and wealth and rise and fall accordingly, or we can love God and love others in kind and just roll with everything life has to offer from there. If we put our trust in eternal things, all will be well.

## Suffering and death

At the heart of the concepts of euthanasia and assisted suicide is the assertion that intentionally causing death is a reasonable and compassionate response to human pain and suffering. As such, I do not believe it is possible to affirm either euthanasia or assisted suicide from within the Christian tradition. It would be misleading, however, to say that Christians are of one mind on this complex issue. Add to the mix arguments about how medical technology has changed the landscape of the debate and it can be difficult to know where to turn.

It is helpful to start with some general definitions. Assisted suicide is the providing of information or the means to take a life. Euthanasia is deliberately killing someone by action or omission, with or without that person's consent, for compassionate reasons. (It is important to realize that withholding or withdrawing medical treatment when its toll outweighs its benefits, giving drugs to relieve pain, even if an unintended effect is to shorten life, or respecting a person's right to refuse or discontinue treatment are not considered to be euthanasia or assisted suicide.)

I share with many others the ambivalent experience of knowing and loving people who suffer pain or illness, live with marked disabilities or linger indefinitely in a vegetative state. My father suffered a stroke in his early forties, and languished in a coma for seventeen long months before he died. The strong desire to bring some kind of immediate, painless resolution to these situations is born from the deep caverns of human love and compassion. We step onto very uncertain ground, however, when the intentional causing of death is permitted as a logical or necessary extension of love and compassion. It is wise to question whether allowing ourselves the option of ending pain or suffering by terminating a person's life represents an achievement or a failure of the human community.

The biblical admonition to "choose life" translates into a call for individuals and communities to provide excellent medical resources and effective moral and practical support to those in need, and to their families. This approach is consistent with the Christian imperative to serve others with compassion, especially those with the greatest needs. To choose life in this manner is to uphold the dignity and worth of every human being, especially when these are being assaulted by pain or suffering or are questioned by the majority's standard for what constitutes quality of life. Many reasoned voices will argue in favour of euthanasia or assisted suicide. However, in choosing to provide wise counsel, effective medicine and consistent care to every person who faces pain suffering or death, we can be certain that we have chosen well.

## Adultery and divorce

Adultery is sexual intercourse involving a person who is married to somebody else (which is different from sexual intercourse between two consenting, unmarried adults). Jesus was unambiguous in his teaching against adultery and saw little distinction between adulterous thoughts and actions. (When a child is born from an adulterous relationship, the circumstances of conception do not detract from a child's place in the eyes of God. All children are equal before God, and all deserve unconditional love, protection and nurture. Some of Jesus' sternest warnings are about protecting children from harm, and he made it clear that to welcome a child is to welcome God.)

The Christian tradition affirms that marriage is a lifelong union of faithful love between a woman and a man, for better and for worse, to the exclusion of all others. Marriage is a gift from God, such that as a woman and a man give themselves to each other in love, and as they grow together and become united in that love, they experience the way God loves. Christian marriage is a sign of God's desire to unite all things in Christ. Marriage does not make people holier or more worthy than others, but those who enter into Christian marriage are called to respect the holiness of their union.

The strong belief that faithful love transforms lives informs the high standards of Christian marriage, and this same belief compels the Church to respond with compassion and understanding when individuals seek to be married a second time. I was profoundly grateful for the total support of my church when I began a new marriage. It would be unfortunate if anyone felt unwelcome because they have experienced the breakdown or ending of a marriage – even those who may have been adulterous in a former marriage. Christian faith has a lot to do with true repentance and forgiveness: Christians are to persevere in resisting evil and, whenever they fall into sin, are encouraged to repent and return to God. The Church is called to uphold both its standards for marriage and its standards for forgiveness and enabling new life.

## Persuasion and evangelism

Christian evangelism – the sharing of the good news of Jesus – has very little to do with clever persuasion, and absolutely nothing to do with inducing or intimidating people. Chapter 13 of St. Paul's Second Letter to the Corinthians describes the qualities of a true evangelist.

Confident Christians understand that if the earth and all its inhabitants are made by God, then evangelism is simply showing the way to the Creator and maker of all. Christians believe that God has been revealed in the person of Jesus, and draws people into faith by the determined power of the Holy Spirit. It is misleading for anyone to think or suggest that their own powers of persuasion or any other tactic will bring someone to truly embrace Christian faith.

Evangelism is not passive, however; it involves proclaiming good news about God and hope for all people. While evangelism has very little to do with cajoling people to say particular words or to start going to a particular church, an evangelist will open a door and point a way for someone to follow – a way that feels liberating and wholesome.

Good news has a good feeling about it, and not everyone responds in the same way to things. Good evangelists are wise and patient, understanding that they may play only a small part in a person's journey, and that whatever they may miss will be provided by God somewhere else along the way.

## Righteous anger

Anger is a complex emotion. Trying to suppress anger or being afraid to express it can lead to even more complex responses, such as depression or self-loathing. If you hold off being angry until you are sure it is truly righteous and acceptable, you might do yourself some harm; it is better to acknowledge your anger when you feel angry, and try to express it in direct and constructive terms.

Jesus demonstrated a range of anger. Knocking over tables and chasing people out of a temple that had been defiled by their commercial ventures is an example of high-end righteous anger, but is a dubious example of socially acceptable behaviour (although it must have been very satisfying for Jesus). Arrogant religious leaders upset Jesus more than once, and he made it clear to them how he felt about their views.

Righteous anger likely has something to do with feeling affronted by actions or situations that violate God's will. However, it is no doubt good to check whether we are angry because others aren't playing by our religious rules, or whether we believe that the Holy Spirit has been aggrieved. In either case, a fit of rage is probably self-serving, while a direct and composed confrontation serves others by allowing them to see clearly the perspective we bring.

## Hatred and virtue

Psalm 19 says that "the Lord loves those who hate evil," and St. Paul wrote in his Letter to the Romans that Christians should "hate what is evil" and "hold fast to what is good." Hatred of some things is virtuous; hatred of other things is not virtuous. For example, hating racial, gender or sexual discrimination is virtuous; hating others because of their race, gender or sexuality is not.

To hate evil is to have an aversion to things that undermine the beauty of creation and crush the esteem of others. To have an aversion to the sexualizing of society – especially of youth – is to love all that is beautiful about human sexuality, and to respect its power to either celebrate or distort human relationships. To dislike the erosion of long-term unions of faithful love is to encourage stable relationships, where conflicts are resolved and reconciliation is made real, modelling for our children how to engage in the stuff of life.

Some distinguish between hating particular behaviours while loving the people involved. This is not a helpful distinction when the behaviour of only one group is targeted, and recipients of behaviour-hating language are unlikely to feel a separation between themselves and what they do. It is probably better to leave such distinctions behind, and to let the notion of "hatred" be something that applies to our own behavioural choices.

When speaking against what others say or do, the term "hatred" brings a tone that is hardly constructive. To speak of what is desirable, just or good is very important, however, and "holding fast" to these things is an active rather than a passive stance. To actively hate anything carries with it the risk of becoming hateful, thereby taking on one of the most undermining aspects of the human spirit. Hatred can be virtuous, but ought not to be considered a virtue.

## War and peace

Peace is not simply the absence of war, and protesting the possibility of war ought not to be confused with condoning the development of weapons of mass destruction or supporting tyrannies. Peace involves living without fear in conditions where food, shelter, clothing, medicine, education and the possibility of self-actualization exist. It is not wrong to strive for, to protect or even to fight for these things.

The Christian tradition holds that although war is at variance with the moral teaching of Jesus, there are conditions where undertaking war is morally defensible. The thirteenth-century theologian and philosopher St. Thomas Aquinas developed St. Augustine's notion of a "just war," which, in a modern formulation, would include these criteria: the cause of the war must be just; there must be some balance between the damage inflicted and the good expected; all other means of solving the conflict must be exhausted; weapons must be controlled; and civilians must not be directly attacked.

I believe that the question of whether war should be pursued is always an urgent religious matter, and that our national leaders can only benefit from a wide range of advice as war is being considered. Our leaders need to see things from the widest and deepest perspectives as they face the horrific decision of whether to place our young men and women in battle.

The Church cannot abdicate its beliefs or its voice as events in the world unfold; neither can our national leaders. We who care about peace must together listen to each other's words and carefully consider whether the case for war is justified. To remain silent is an untenable option when the stakes are so high, and our leaders do not deserve to be left alone when pondering such grave matters.

## Terror and paradise

The notion of earthly delights being a reward in heaven is a dangerous perversion if it is held out as an incentive to do something as appalling as killing others and oneself for the sake of political and ideological gains. I would state in the strongest terms that terrorism of any order can in no way be justified or explained by religion. Such actions are purely a function of human political ideology, and to use religious language to persuade people to support or commit terrorist acts is an affront to all people of faith and conscience.

Christianity doesn't promise earthly delights on earth, let alone in heaven. In fact, the eternal values of love, hope, peace and reconciliation have very little to do with things like lots of sex, shopping or even sunny days. In many cases, pursuing eternal values comes at the cost of creature delights – serving God ideally places others' needs before our own.

God is love, and human beings are made in the image of God. God does not lead people to acts of terror; hatred is contrary to God's nature. Every human person is capable of allowing themselves to be influenced by other people's ideas and to follow whatever is deemed to be "right," and people will forever clash and kill over borders and loyalties. This is not God's will, and has no place in the language of any faith; this is the language of rulers and regimes, not of religion.

Heaven is a place of rest, of life everlasting, where sorrow, pain and sighs are no more. It is a place where mercy and grace are given and received, where broken souls find peace and wholeness, and where there is no exploitation and fear. God's light and love will pervade everyone and everything, and enemies will sit side by side. Heaven can touch and transform life on earth when human wills are aligned with God's will and acts of kindness and forgiveness exceed acts of violence and vengeance.

## A day of rest

The biblical concept of Sabbath derives from the rest God took on the seventh day after the work of Creation. The books of Exodus and Deuteronomy establish the Sabbath as a day to be sanctified by solemn rest and worship, beginning at sundown on Friday and lasting until sundown on Saturday.

Many of the earliest Christians continued to observe the Jewish Sabbath as a day of rest and prayer. However, the first day of the week, Sunday, gradually became the focus for the early Church. Sunday was the "Lord's Day," the day Christ rose from the dead, and the day when the Holy Spirit was given to his followers, enabling them to publicly proclaim his resurrection for the first time.

In the early Church, Sunday was often called the "eighth day," suggesting that the work of Creation ended with Christ: God created for six days, rested on the seventh, and completed the work of Creation on the eighth day. In other words, Sunday represented the renewal of the world in Christ, the start of a new creation. Sunday consequently became the principal day to celebrate the "Lord's Supper," where Christians received the new life of

Christ in bread and wine that had been taken, blessed and shared as Jesus had commanded.

For contemporary Christians, Sunday continues to be a holy day, set apart by people of faith to commemorate the joy of the resurrection and to celebrate the new life that is freely given to the whole of creation. It is a day to draw together the strands of the week, to relinquish all that is destructive and to receive what is truly good. Sunday is when Christians gather together as the Church, as communities of believers, to taste the mystery of God, to remember their destiny as children of God, and to be strengthened again for the task of serving in the world God loves.

## Pilgrimages

Pilgrimages traditionally involve going to a holy place for reasons of devotion, to obtain some kind of spiritual help, or as an act of penance. Pilgrimages, especially pilgrimages to the Holy Land, are a common part of the Christian tradition. The idea of being in the actual places where Jesus was, or following the footsteps of the apostles, has a certain attraction for Christians, and many who take such pilgrimages find them to be life-changing.

Christians are not obligated to make pilgrimages, but are encouraged to listen when their spirits are restless, and to consider what is beckoning. For some this may mean making a pilgrimage, if not to the Holy Land, then to somewhere that helps bring a renewed sense of faith or direction.

To set out on any kind of journey, some degree of comfort and security is sacrificed for the sake of being able to move about more freely. Pilgrimages can begin with apprehension or enthusiasm, and much of being on a pilgrimage involves letting go of what is unnecessary so you can come to see what is truly necessary.

There is a 12-kilometre stretch of beach on the eastern shore of New Brunswick where I have walked many times, watching my children grow, skipping stones, and allowing thoughts to sort and sift. With each visit this long walk took on greater significance, as memories and possibilities for the future mingled with hopes and fears. Those visits ended unexpectedly with the sudden ending of my marriage. I do not know if I will walk that beach again, but if I do, it will be a pilgrimage that brings to mind what every part of life's journey has taught me: that God is at the beginning and at the end of every path, and that hope is never far away. I believe this is what pilgrimages are meant to do.

# 4

# Is there faith in the world around me?

Sometimes we hear indignant voices bemoaning the abandonment of faith in the public, secular realm – as though, at one time, Canadian society was uniformly religious. I remember singing hymns and saying the Lord's Prayer every morning when I was a boy in public school on the prairies: attendance was compulsory but conviction was not a requirement. Custom and the presumption of (Christian) faith – the values of the dominant group, more likely – determined the practice. Perhaps it is only the appearance of religious conviction that has been lost.

So, is there faith in the world around us? Perhaps it is better to ask when it is reasonable to express faith in the world at large, and where and when expressions of faith should be expected. Looking for faith "out there" may, in the end, be much less satisfying than seeking faith in the place where religious conviction is born: within.

## Challenges to faith

How nice it would be to have faith bolstered by constant affirmations, encouragement and support in schools, the marketplace and the workplace, by the media and in the corridors of power. Instead, there is a wariness (sometimes wavering) between the influence of society and the influence of the sacred. If one is seen to be too much affected by the other, notes of caution sound – perhaps because of the potential for either one to use the other for dubious purposes.

Three developments that affect and challenge religious faith are secularism, pluralism and relativism. Secularism is the prevalence of perspectives or ways of being that are not "religious." Pluralism suggests the presence of many perspectives or beliefs, some religious and some not. Relativism occurs when the authority of one set of beliefs is diminished by deference to another, more attractive way of being.

In Canada, religious belief tends to be expressed privately, and church attendance figures suggest that many are not actively part of a faith community. Christian denominations in Canada often differ greatly on points including the interpretation of scripture, morality or assertions about God, and, along with others who seek to influence what people believe, are in themselves part of a more pervasive pluralism in our society. Other trends suggest that behaviour, whether individual or collective, tends to be governed less by a careful seeking of what is "right" or "just" than by what is pragmatic or expedient.

Churches respond to these challenges in ways that range from insular and reactionary to trendy and diffuse. The Anglican Church is conscious of and committed to its rich connection to the very beginnings of Christianity, and is intentionally comprehensive in nature, encompassing a breadth of orthodox liturgical and theological perspectives within a single worldwide communion. This, coupled with a strong ministry of practical service and a willingness to seek dialogue and co-operation with others, enables it to be relevant for many people in many different contexts. It also allows a democratic form of governance to coexist with the authority of its bishops, ensuring that many voices are heard as it seeks to discern and faithfully respond to the mind of Christ in challenging times.

With its long history and distinctive ethos, rapid change is not a dominant feature of the Anglican Church. Some people find this frustrating, especially when the challenges of secularism, pluralism and relativism appear to demand significant changes. Given the nature of these challenges, however, it is probably wiser to effect change in a manner that avoids the pitfall of discarding things that are eternal and necessary in favour of things that are simply expeditious in the particular circumstances of the present time.

## The secular state

The definition of a state as "secular" suggests that while political ideologies can influence citizens, religions cannot – at least not in public institutions. This appears to mean that the state and its institutions (and symbols) are the principal terms under which people unite as a nation.

While at least one country has passed legislation forbidding students from wearing Muslim head scarves, large crucifixes, yarmulkes and other religious symbols in public schools, in Canada expressions of faith are encouraged as part of the multicultural fabric of our society. By recognizing the importance of faith as part of culture, and by allowing many and diverse cultures to be given equal recognition and respect, we seem to be enabling co-operation and coexistence. This is reasonable and constructive legislation.

There is another way of seeing things, however. A country that obviously removes references to religion appears to be diminishing the influence of religion. Canada, by obviously recognizing its multi-faith nature, appears to be enhancing religion, but is probably more interested in promoting benign cultural diversity than in enfranchising religions and allowing them to influence public policy.

On one hand, a multicultural or multi-faith policy recognizes and encourages harmony and acceptance of differences in a diverse society; on the other hand, multiculturalism is a pragmatic and entirely secular way of managing the influence of religion.

By developing a policy of multiculturalism that recognizes religion as a key part of culture, we are likely building a society that is, in effect, no less secular than countries that downplay religion. Multiculturalism is a secular vehicle that addresses religious diversity, acknowledging its different parts but subsuming them into a neutral whole, state-sanctioned and palatable for all.

## Faith at school

I wonder what purpose is served when private religious schools choose not to hire a teacher of another tradition. Unless the subject matter involves religious instruction, it strikes me as odd that a school of any order would not seek out and hire the very best teachers, regardless of religious belief. If religious schools, whether fully funded by government or not, aim to be places of engendering uniform religious belief by like-minded instructors, then one must ask whether this is good for society as a whole.

Given the richness and creativity that diversity can produce, and given also the need for greater understanding and communication between and within the world's religious, cultural and national communities, our children can only benefit from studying with people who support different political parties and who have diverse religious, racial and ethnic origins. Even though the many publicly-funded Roman Catholic schools in Canada have historically held to a policy of hiring Catholics, I still believe that schools serving a single constituency that hire beyond that constituency provide a richer forum for learning, a forum where differences are understood by actually meeting and learning together.

God's creation is diverse, and this is very good. Christians believe that God loves the world so much that Christ gave his life as a sign of God's faithful love: that all people on earth would be reconciled and live in peace and goodwill. Our schools should be for everyone, places where goodness of every kind can be recognized and celebrated without fear.

## Counselling in high schools

In 1985, the Toronto Board of Education published a compendium of information from eleven religions and from secular humanism called *Readings and Prayers for Use in Toronto Schools*. The document contends that "all students should have the opportunity to see their traditions as part of school life," and it sought to enable students and teachers "to learn more about classmates and students sitting respectively next to, and before, them." The sage advice given is that affirming spirituality and allowing people to become familiar with the beliefs of others can strengthen rather than divide communities.

High-school students should be able to benefit from pastoral care as part of student services in general. Guidance counsellors who are concerned about addressing the needs of students from a holistic perspective should know when to suggest spiritual guidance and have a list of qualified clergy who are available for referrals.

Having a trained chaplain who visits the school regularly might be possible in some cases, but that person must realize that those who seek counsel may not share (or may not want to share) the same faith. Some students may simply want to take a theologically trained person to task on how or why anybody could believe in God. Others may be asking searching questions about the divine, or may be confused about issues in their lives that conflict with their religious beliefs. Still others may want some advice on finding a faith community or religious tradition that speaks to them.

Regardless of where a chaplain or pastoral counsellor meets students, the purpose must be to provide safe ways of exploring spiritual questions. It would be most inappropriate if pastoral care in a high-school context was seen as an opportunity to proselytize or give religious instruction, nor should it attempt to set up one faith against another. Affirming spirituality as an integral part of a person's overall well-being can do a great service to the development of mature, open and self-aware adults.

## Modernizing the faith

Many people appear to harbour a broadly defined fear of abandoning "traditional religious teachings." Thinking in terms of values, rituals and beliefs can help us consider belief and change in more specific ways.

Values change over time. Slavery was once condoned, now it is not; women were once considered to be property, now they are not; usury was condemned in the Bible, but most Christians freely participate in an economic system based on money loaned for interest; human sexuality was once seen in monochrome, functional, reproductive terms, now it is not. Clearly, values can change and are shaped by the interplay of belief and social change. This is likely to continue as it always has, and we must be ever watchful of the moral relativism that looms large in society.

Rituals also change over time. Praying in a language that people no longer speak or understand has been rightly changed to the vernacular. Worship spaces can be reconfigured, music can be modernized, and ritual gestures can be modified without affecting core beliefs. Familiarity is a key part of ritual, however, and constant change can undermine some of its sublime aspects. If it is modified purely for the sake of appealing to contemporary sensibilities, worship may feel more like a hyped-up political rally than an act of communion with the timeless, transcendent Creator of Creation.

The core beliefs of Christianity are crystallized in its ancient creeds, and these beliefs do not change over time. Abandoning these beliefs is a fool's game, especially if it is done to appear more modern and inclusive; appearance matters little in the absence of substance. Christianity has revealed truths that are fundamental: the long-term effect of abandoning these truths would result in faith being replaced by a shallow and contrived religion that becomes increasingly ill-defined as new notions of modernity and inclusiveness cross its path – and impaired in its ability to make wise decisions about its values and rituals.

## Religion and politics

Churches are not private societies that exist independently from the world around them. Members of churches are also members of society and freely engage in positions of leadership and influence in the public arena. I would hope that people of faith struggle with the difficult task of trying to be true to God in the many places they live, work and play.

The question of whether religions should be involved in social or political issues is somewhat more complex. Any discipline brings a unique perspective to discussions of our common life. Professional associations, unions, non-governmental organizations, business lobbies and commercial banks all participate in the to and fro of debate that affects how decisions are made. Religious organizations represent a majority of Canadians, and it is perfectly reasonable for their leaders to enter into debate or commentary on issues that affect the common good. By the same token, these contributions must be subject to the same assessment as other bodies that are working to influence opinion or action.

If a religious organization seeks to influence the policies of government, the presentation of how religious belief bears on specific issues must be supported by accurate information on the situation. Sometimes religious groups fail to grasp the nuances of an issue and are quickly dismissed; often, however, religious leaders or coalitions have done their homework and astute analysis and argument clearly demonstrate the relevance of their perspective.

Eternal and noble ideals are nearly always compromised in the attempt to address the needs of particular times and places. There is a fine line between religion and ideology, and the two often blend into one. Religious bodies are a part of the world and care deeply for the well-being of creation. Rather than hiding from the world, they attempt to bring peace and goodwill by trying to reconcile eternal ideals with the realities of the world we all share. We ought to be wary of anyone who suggests that religion easily translates into law or social programs; however, religious leaders or organizations have every right to lend their voices and perspectives to conversations that seek to benefit the well-being of all people.

## God and the constitution

The debate over whether there ought to be a reference to God in the Canadian constitution appears to have very little to do with its efficacy. Some voices seem to use the debate as a platform either to discredit or to defend faith in God. Other voices seem to believe that removing or keeping the reference to God is a personal affront, a sign of moral decay or a great symbolic victory. Different parties seem concerned that the presence or absence of the name of God in the constitution threatens them, as though one side will win at the expense of the other.

Those who want to remove the reference cannot change the fundamental structure of reality, just as those who want to keep the reference cannot expect all to subscribe to the same faith. People who are secure in their beliefs, whether religious or not, tend not to get upset about legal documents unless justice is obviously not being served. Since the debate over keeping the reference to God in the constitution is not about the corruption of justice, it has become a tiresome and at times vindictive harangue that embarrasses sensible people.

I do not believe that keeping a reference to God in the constitution makes Canada a "faithful" nation, nor do I believe that removing the reference makes it an atheistic nation. Words on a page are of little consequence unless they reflect or inspire human lives.

The constitution is fundamentally a practical legal document that attempts to name and defer to high ideals and profound goodness for the sake of our country and its citizens. God is a living presence who creates time and space and is present to the whole course of human history, whether named in a constitution or not.

## The Charter and morality

Basic morality suggests the fundamental criteria we might use to determine what kind of people we ought to be and what kinds of things we ought to do. Some people question whether the Charter of Rights and Freedoms is causing us to abandon some kind of shared moral code. It is possible to speak about some of the issues involved in this question from a Christian perspective.

Although Christianity is not, first and foremost, a moral code, we believe that the revelation of God in Christ invites individuals to respond in ways that may be called moral. In other words, who we are to be is based on who we understand Jesus to be, and what we are called to do is guided by what Jesus did. As children of God, we are compelled to bring the virtues of God into our own lives and the life of the world around us. These virtues include the steadfast care and protection of those who are most vulnerable.

Generally speaking, the Canadian Charter of Rights and Freedoms is something to be proud of. Among other things, it allows for the weighing of public interest against the rights and freedoms of the individual. However, in the case of a 1999 British Columbia Supreme Court ruling that has given new vehemence to questions about the "morality" of the Charter, a judge has argued that it is not in the public interest to limit an individual's right to possess child pornography.

A curious feature of this ruling is the fact that the material in question is indisputably child pornography. In other words, it seems to be saying that an individual has the right to possess images of anybody's children in sexually explicit situations. As a father of three, I find that even the suggestion stirs a strong, primal instinct in me to resist such a point of view in order to protect all our children.

We do well to question whether this ruling is moral, let alone just. Something is profoundly wrong if the most vulnerable members of our society are not completely protected from exploitation. The production or possession of child pornography is in no way consistent with God's will for children – or for anybody else.

The outrage that has been expressed by many people over this ruling suggests that some basic moral sense has been violated. Thankfully, we live in a country that allows public interest, within a reasonable degree, to override individual rights. This is more likely to happen when people of faith and conscience consider the basis for their most deeply held beliefs and act accordingly to oppose what they believe to be immoral.

## Social welfare and the churches

Christians work in every part of society and are called by their baptism to serve Christ in all people. The inherent humanism of the Christian tradition speaks to the highest goals of government, and believes that the state ought to be the primary vehicle for caring for those who require social assistance. A just society would meet the needs of those who are most vulnerable, offering a "preferential option for the poor" that is borne out in the normal functioning of elected governments and their bureaucracies. It would be good to live in a place where altruistic values are part of the social contract: where no person needs to look any farther than the state for appropriate assistance, citizens are taxed in such a way that sufficient resources can be made available to get at the core causes of need, these causes are addressed as thoroughly as possible, and the residual needs of any person who cannot live without social assistance are met.

It would appear as though governments in our country have encouraged the devolution of social assistance to the community sector. As a result, volunteer organizations and churches now engage in extensive social welfare ministries. Some people are keen to be involved in these ministries; we are, after all, meant to be altruistic and to care for the vulnerable and the needy in our midst.

However, as this devolution of care happens, faith groups should resist the temptation to simply pick up social assistance work, and in some cases should refuse to participate in anything that is remotely suggestive of the days when the Church was the caretaker of the poor and needy. We ought to expect the state to espouse our values as a compassionate society and to allocate tax dollars accordingly. We live in an affluent country and if all people, irrespective of belief, seek to ensure that our governments take on the highest human values, then the work of enabling and caring for those who are most needy can be shared by all citizens. Whether through taxation or through serving in well-funded social assistance programs and facilities, the work of tending to those most in need would be met by everyone, rather than being subtly downloaded to the community sector.

## Religion and ethnic identity

If ethnic identity is determined by those aspects of culture that distinguish one group from another, and if religion is seen to be a part of culture, then religion can both contribute to and help preserve ethnic identity. Whether religion is *intended* to preserve ethnic identity is another matter altogether.

Religious experience finds expression in culture. When people experience faith in a force other than themselves, the experience is invariably brought to language, art, politics or economics, where it may be received by others and may eventually evolve into a system of beliefs and practices that is passed from one generation to another. It is also possible for the same religion to find expression in different cultures. The Anglican Communion, for example, represents Christian faith that is multilingual and multicultural.

Because religion deals with issues of deepest meaning, it can become a central part of a culture and a significant determinant of ethnic identity. When a culture engenders an identity that reflects the virtues of true religious experience, such as altruism and life-affirming meaning, then all is well. But when a culture contributes to a self-serving or destructive posture, then religion may become a counter-cultural force that challenges aspects of ethnic identity.

The purpose of religion is to enable people to taste the divine and to inspire them to live meaningful and constructive lives, not to preserve ethnic identity. Although those who accept God's love and grace may express their faith in a specific culture, they find their true identity in God.

## Finding common ground

In the early 1960s, Paul Tillich, the renowned theologian and philosopher, gave a number of lectures at Columbia University on "Christianity and the Encounter of the World Religions." He saw "God" as an unnecessary element in defining religion. Tillich writes, "Religion is the state of being grasped by an ultimate concern, a concern which qualifies all other concerns as primary and which itself contains the answer to the question of the meaning of life."

Although Tillich recognizes that "God" is the predominant religious name for such an "ultimate concern," he shows that non-theistic religions often ascribe divine qualities to a sacred object or a high principle. He goes further to suggest that there are "secular" religions where nation, science, a type of society or some other ideal are "elevated to unlimited ultimacy."

Religions – as Tillich defines them – differ on the nature of "God" and what "God" wants from us, because history has produced very different notions of what the "ultimate concern" is, and people have been prepared to sacrifice other concerns that are in conflict with theirs. The result has been competition between religions (be they theistic, non-theistic or secular), rather than the carving out of common ground.

By their nature, religions seek to define "us" and "them": those who are grasped by the same ultimate concern, and those who are not. The extent to which faith enables us to transcend this tendency to "tribalism" is a sign of spiritual maturity. In the end, if God is either revealed or understood to be the Creator of life, then seeking to weave together those strands of faith and life that bring creation into constructive unity is a laudable, if not ultimate, concern.

## The faith of politicians

I suspect that there are politicians who believe that their religious beliefs should influence their decision-making. This is perfectly fair. One of the most penetrating questions for religious people is how their faith affects the way they live. Ideally, politicians who have faith struggle with the difficult task of trying to be true to God in the political arena. For most politicians, this is a personal matter, and, thankfully, we live in a country where religion does not need to be declared by people who wish to run in an election.

If, however, a politician intends (or purports) to devise policies that operationalize his or her religious beliefs, then that person should declare his or her intentions. It is debatable whether anyone knows how to bring about a "Christian" society (for example) or a "liberal" or "conservative" society. In the end, most successful politicians or governing parties will use some combination of wisdom and expediency, along with pure pragmatism, to produce policies that may or may not be distinctive from any other person or party, religious or not.

Politicians of faith would do well simply to deal faithfully with the tasks at hand, always seeking to reconcile noble ideals with the exigencies of the place and people they govern. If faith helps politicians do their work well, give glory to God, but remember that religion is not the same as social policy, and it is wise to be cautious of anyone who suggests otherwise.

## Religion and political decisions

Leaders use all kinds of reasons to explain or justify their decisions, and in a free and democratic society, people can accept or criticize whatever rationale politicians use. However, if people are not free to express dissenting views, then it matters little whether religion, ideology or blind ambition is the motive for political leadership.

Freedom of speech and the right to elect leaders on the basis of transparent political, social and economic agendas are what truly matters. If a party or a person runs for office having fully disclosed a specific religion-based agenda, then people ought to be free to decide whether election is deserved. Bringing in religion after the fact is a little dubious, and people may well criticize someone for doing so.

Ideally, religious commentary ought to be something that measures whether political actions or decisions are just, rather than a justification for such matters. However, if a political leader's platform is obviously based on a particular religion, why not use the tenets of that religion to guide or justify actions? In the end, we can all be assured that God sides with the truth.

## Public prayer

I am always happy to respond to invitations to pray at public events. Although I assume that people want a person of a certain faith to pray, I do not assume that everyone present shares or wants to share the same faith. And while I may choose to use a form of prayer that draws from a wide range of orthodox pronouns or adjectives, I cannot pray in a generic way to an anonymous god. As a Christian,

I can only pray from my experience of faith in the God of Jesus Christ; it would be impossible or false for me to pray otherwise.

The purpose of prayer is to express adoration or thanksgiving, to intercede on behalf of others or to seek God's guidance for oneself. Prayer is not a sermon or religious instruction, nor is it a way to set up one faith against another. The purpose of public prayer is not to proselytize, but to acknowledge and invite the presence of the divine. Some who listen may share this belief and others may not, but no one should feel that they are being preached to. Properly understanding prayer and allowing people to become familiar with the faith of others can strengthen rather than divide communities.

Wise people know that it is God who sifts and guides the hearts of others, and that being true to our faith means treating others as we would like to be treated. People who are confident in their faith have every reason to live out their faith in a manner that is generous and respectful, certain that God, who loves them, is quite capable of loving everybody else.

## The meaning of life

James Carroll, an American author and columnist, considering remarks about Islam made by a senior U.S. military officer, writes, "The ethical dilemma facing all religions today, but perhaps especially religions of revelation, is laid bare here: How to affirm one's own faith without denigrating the faith of others?" (*Boston Globe*, October 23, 2003).

How can we say that our faith provides the "best answer" to the meaning of life without falling into the dangerous game of contempt and violence that wreaks havoc in many parts of our world?

Christian scripture provides a basic answer to this question. Jesus said: "Whoever believes in me believes not in me but in him who sent me. And whoever sees me sees him who sent me"; and "Take my yoke upon you, and learn from me; for I am gentle and humble in heart, and you will find rest for your souls."

To a person who didn't understand everything he talked about, Jesus simply said, "You are close to the kingdom of God"; to all who would listen he said, "Love one another." In chapter 4 of the Letter to the Philippians we read: "Whatever is true, whatever is honourable, whatever is just, whatever is pure, whatever is pleasing, whatever is commendable, if there is any excellence and anything worthy of praise, think about these things."

Peaceful coexistence and co-operation are just and commendable things to think about. Because Jesus Christ also walked and suffered on this earth, his words give balance to such thinking: "Be wise as serpents and innocent as doves"; and "I came that everyone may have life, and have it abundantly." While many of us may not quite grasp the meaning of life, striving to help people have meaningful lives probably moves everyone a bit closer to the kingdom of God.

# 5

# Why go to church?

Everybody, religious or not, should ask this question at least once in their lives. It makes sense to say "Why bother?" if belief in God or belonging to a religion doesn't make any difference. If you can see why it matters, then it makes equal sense to do all you can to strengthen and celebrate your faith within a church community.

I go to church because I am thankful. But I can understand why a person who sees going to church as a dreary duty might question its importance. If you are new to the whole business, church can seem a bit intimidating, if not strange. However, if you find the worship uplifting, if the people are friendly, and if there are opportunities to grow in faith and to serve others, then going to church can make all the difference in the world.

Although I have always had some kind of belief in God and have always been connected to the Anglican Church, there was a time when I chose to be apart – a time when I honestly could not see that belief in God or belonging to a church made any difference at all.

Once, during that time, I was confronted by the consequences of human inconsistency and a disturbing sense of how fleeting are the things we build up around ourselves. Feeling quite alone, I cried out in defiant anger to what I had been told was God. To my utter surprise, God was there, and I was filled with a profound sense of peace. I was both silenced and comforted, led forward again by a gentle, mighty presence.

What began to draw me back to faith, and to the church, was the quiet conviction that in the midst of life is a bracing, benevolent and challenging force that is independent of everything else. None of the many trying moments in my life have been able to diminish this conviction.

The language of the Christian tradition gives expression to my conviction: in the life, death and resurrection of Jesus we are told that God is with us, visiting us with the Holy Spirit, and offering to us possibilities, even when there appear to be no possibilities at all. To grasp this, however tentatively, is to understand what salvation is all about.

## Do we need religion?

In order to make sense of the world, humans develop systems of symbols, such as language. The various sounds or gestures that humans can make are structured in such a way that groups of people can communicate with one another. Human beings normally survive in groups, so shared symbols are needed.

As new phenomena are introduced into the experience of a group, new symbols are formed. When a phenomenon is fundamentally new, like Abraham's first encounter with the Lord God, language expands to capture and relay the experience to others. Words about Jesus came about after people experienced his life, death and resurrection. Christianity is therefore understood to be a revealed religion.

I think it is inaccurate to say humans need religion. Religion is not a need; it is something that has naturally emerged in human societies. In other words, some religions may be purely cultural, drawn together by the particular situation of one group of people; others transcend cultures and historical situations and point to eternal things that speak to all people.

## Personal religious experience

If you are a person of faith, then your personal religious experience is very important. Faith is, in very simple terms, a person's relationship with God. If you can't speak at some level about a personal experience of God, it would be difficult to say you have a relationship with God. Since faith is about your relationship with God, personal religious experience is pretty fundamental stuff, and needs to be given careful consideration.

Christian faith flows from personal experience, but is never to be completely private. Like any relationship, faith in God through Christ is something that changes over time, and can be simple and clear or complex and many-layered. This means that personal religious experience constantly needs to be brought into the discerning light of others in the Christian community, where the experience can be understood and supported, and where misperceptions or distortions can be more clearly seen.

Balance is always important in spiritual matters. The interplay of personal experience with the experience of the whole Church enables each person to consider their understanding of God's purpose alongside proved wisdom. In the Christian tradition, personal religious experience is ideally weighed against and woven into the living faith of others, with due regard for scripture and tradition.

## When church is boring

You do not need to attend church to be a believer, but you do need to participate regularly in the worship and ministry of a church to actually be a member of it. Saying you are a member of a church you have nothing to do with is a bit like saying you are married while living completely separate from your partner.

If you find worship boring and not enlightening, first ask yourself what you seek when you go to church. Then ask what is missing in either your church's life or in your own everyday life.

Is everything boring and not enlightening? What aspect of your church's life that interests you could you participate in, such as a study group, a choir or some ministry of service? How can you get to know individuals in the congregation? Have you spoken to the pastor about your feelings?

If a particular church doesn't give you what you think you need, then try somewhere else. Since the very beginning there has been a diversity of churches, and you might find what you seek in another community.

Try not to be simply a spectator or a passerby, though – you really have to make an attempt to become part of a new church, meeting others halfway. And try not to place too much emphasis on assessing the merits of the priest or pastor: you will never find an omni-competent individual to meet all your needs. Look instead at the community as a whole. A good church has lots of people involved in making things interesting and enlightening – and many of those people are probably looking for the same things you are on a Sunday morning.

## Breaking bread together

The Anglican Church encourages and welcomes all Christians who have been baptized to receive communion during celebrations of the Holy Eucharist. The affirmation "one Lord, one Faith, one Baptism" describes our understanding that if it is the Lord's Table, then all who have been baptized into the faith are welcome to receive the Lord's Supper.

The Eucharist is a meal that nurtures the spirit by feeding all the senses – like a dinner party drawn together by a warm and gracious host, where sound, space, touch and taste are at once stimulating and serene. Celebrating the Eucharist is a time to offer and receive, to understand and be understood – a gentle, wonderful banquet.

As a foretaste of God's will for humankind, the Eucharist is profoundly symbolic: God provides the same food at the same table for all who choose to receive. It matters little who you are at the Lord's Table: we are utterly equal in God's eyes, and we receive equally from God.

The Eucharist is about God providing real, spiritual food to children, women and men. To receive Christ in the simple, timeless elements of bread and wine is to receive the eternal, redeeming and transforming love of God. To take and eat this bread and to drink from this cup is to allow ourselves to share in the eternal life of the Creator of Creation.

# Tithing

A tithe is one tenth of something. Some people believe that tithing – giving ten per cent of their income as an offering to God through the Church – is consistent with certain passages in the Bible, and that this is normative. Others suggest that our system of state taxation and social welfare makes giving ten per cent to the Church excessive, and choose instead to give ten per cent of their income to a variety of charitable organizations, including their church.

An accountant friend of mine likes to say that "numbers tell stories." Looking at a spreadsheet of your finances over the course of a year and considering where you devote your dollars can say a lot about what you value most. Most people seem to give about one per cent of their income to the Church. Imagine what would be achieved if everybody gave even two per cent to the ministry of the Church. Imagine if they gave ten per cent.

In practical terms, money is essential to any church, and members are encouraged to give conscientiously, ensuring that the Church is not encumbered by deficits or debts, and that there is freedom to respond to new opportunities or needs that arise. There is no set amount requested from each individual, but the Church attempts to clearly communicate its financial requirements and to show that its revenues are used responsibly to glorify God. It is important for people to know what they are supporting when they give to their church, and if they can see the good works it accomplishes, then it is natural for people to feel good about supporting it.

In spiritual terms, God wants our entire life to be one of devotion to everything that God loves. Giving money to the Church is only one part of living out a life of faith and commitment, and is in many ways much easier than serving Christ in all persons and respecting the dignity of every human being. For Christians, offering money to God through the Church ought to be an extension of offering our whole self to following the way of Jesus, which is, in essence, a one hundred per cent gift to God.

## Commitment to the faith

The faith of the Anglican Church is communicated through its worship. For example, the Sunday Eucharist normally opens with this prayer: "Almighty God, unto whom all hearts are open, all desires known, and from whom no secrets are hidden; cleanse the thoughts of our hearts by the inspiration of your Holy Spirit, that we may perfectly love you, and worthily magnify your glorious name, through Christ our Lord. Amen." This prayer makes an encompassing statement about the nature of God and our relationship to God, through Christ, by the power of the Holy Spirit.

I don't know what percentage of Anglicans are wholeheartedly committed to and guided by their relationship to God, as taught in this particular prayer. I do know that most seem to pass on regular worship, and are as prone as everyone else to latching onto odd notions of the Christian faith that abound outside the teaching of the Church.

For example, a recent bestselling book depicts a world view that has God planning every detail of each person's life. A high-grossing film presents a manipulative and contrived story of the last days of Jesus. I can only imagine the range of conclusions readers of that book may reach concerning God's "plan" for their lives, and I hope more people base their faith on Christ's passion and resurrection as they are expressed in the Bible.

Because so many voices attempt to say what the Christian way is all about – for good or for ill – it is important for Christians to be nurtured in and to follow the faith as it comes through the worship of the Church, where Christ is proclaimed in ways that have been proven trustworthy.

## Dissenting

The Anglican tradition enjoys much diversity and debate, with dissenting views regularly expressed – and occasionally acted on. Anglicanism is guided by the constant interplay of the Word of God, the accumulated wisdom and practice of the Church, and the discerning minds of each new generation of Christians. Dissent is part of the development of the Church through time, generating dialectics that often change the way the Church responds to situations.

For the most part, dissenting voices cause the Church to reflect more carefully on the faith it carries. Dissent is normally not suppressed or discouraged, and as long as the dissenting person or group doesn't stop worshipping with others in the Anglican Communion, the consequence has been simply to hold very different views within one communion. The bond is the faith that is expressed in the liturgy of the Church through authorized, successive forms of common prayer.

In other words, if dissenters can, in good conscience, still worship with the Church – or remain in communion with the Church – then they are still of the Church, even if their ideas about the faith may be extraordinary. It is by remaining in or removing oneself from communion with others that assent or dissent is ultimately measured. To worship with the Church, despite holding a dissenting view, is to assent to the faith of the Church; to remove oneself from communion with the Church is to express dissent as an action that is more than the absence of assent, and reveals its own consequences.

## Gay Sunday School teachers

Finding volunteers to teach in a church school is not always easy, although the work is as rewarding as it is demanding. It is a great privilege to be involved in opening the scriptures to children and providing them with a safe and nurturing environment where they can feel and participate in God's empowering and challenging love. It is a ministry some people are uniquely called to, and it is the duty of each congregation to consider carefully anyone who volunteers to serve in this way.

The Anglican Church of Canada affirms the presence and contributions of gay men and lesbians in the life of the church, and condemns bigotry, violence and hatred directed towards anyone because of their sexual orientation. This means that sexual orientation should not be the basis for accepting or refusing someone who volunteers to teach in a church school.

However, there are two basic requirements for anyone who volunteers to teach children in an Anglican parish. First, the person must be a well-known, responsible and committed member of the parish community in order to be entrusted with the education and safety of its children. Second, the person should demonstrate a mature Christian faith and a genuine ability to teach children in a manner consistent with Anglican doctrine and worship.

Because the well-being of children is a primary concern of parishes, someone who fails to satisfy these two requirements should not be considered for teaching church school. On the other hand, someone who meets these requirements should be encouraged and supported in this important ministry.

## Worshipping elsewhere

Anyone is welcome to attend services in an Anglican church, and it is permissible for Christians to attend services in other places of worship. Customs may vary across other religions and denominations, however, and it might be wise to see whether the place you plan on attending has the same policy.

I would be curious to know why someone would wish to attend worship in an entirely different religion. If the reason is to develop an appreciation for a diversity of religious traditions, then so be it; being firmly grounded in our own religious tradition allows us to affirm what is good in others, and there is nothing wrong with that.

If you are uncertain of what to believe and seek to explore many traditions in order to find a spiritual home, then it makes sense to look objectively at what is around. If you are spiritually needy, you may be easily influenced by those who seek to proselytize newcomers or visitors. Some religious bodies are highly skilled at drawing in vulnerable people. It takes time to see what makes a religion tick, and careful discernment is always required in affairs of the spirit.

Faith is usually not something a person turns off and on, or, like a television, something where the channels can change when you like. Living out our faith normally includes being involved in a community and its traditions and beliefs, such as a specific church, mosque or synagogue. To actually be a member, by whatever rite of initiation, of two or more religious traditions (such as some combination of Christianity, Judaism or Islam) would require very fluid thinking, and would probably mean that you are missing a few important bits here and there.

In a world where religion is often used to divide people, appreciation and understanding between the long-established religions of the world is urgent and essential. At the same time, nurturing a distinct spirituality is integral to being fully human, and it is not possible to be completely clinical and objective when it comes to choosing where or how to worship. There are deviations and differences between (and within) religions, and this cannot be ignored. In the end, true religion calls individuals and communities to express love of God by loving others.

## Planning a wedding

During a wedding ceremony two people make solemn, lifelong vows. It is important to be sure that you are comfortable with what you are asked to say and do. Depending on where you get married, it may be more or less possible to accommodate the different perspectives you and your partner bring to the ceremony. A groom may make his vows according to his tradition while the bride uses words that reflect her convictions. Alternatively, the rules of the church you marry in may require that you both follow a prescribed form. A meeting with the person who is to officiate at the wedding should answer your question about options, and, if the person is sensible, should help you both feel comfortable with whatever ceremony is proposed.

It may be wise, however, to ask yourself whether any discomfort you feel is simply about the choice of wedding ceremony. You and your future spouse need to have a broad discussion about the place of religion in your lives and how you plan to share that with any children you may have before you choose when, where or how to be married. Faith normally includes being involved in a community of faith, such as a parish or congregation. Similarly, a non-religious philosophy of life can have a profound effect on the way a person lives. Your convictions or your partner's religious faith may come to influence much more than your wedding ceremony.

If you have not already done so, you may want to step back from planning your wedding and have a good listen to one another's views. Talk about what you believe and what has caused you to hold these beliefs. Ask what place these beliefs have for you as individuals, and what place they may have in your life as a couple, or as a family. Listen carefully to the depth and strength of one another's convictions. If you find that you understand, respect and can accommodate each other's views, then you probably can sort out the details of your wedding ceremony. If you find that your differing views generate more feelings of discomfort or unhappy disagreement, you may need to take some time before proceeding. In either case, take heart. This could be a great opportunity to deepen your relationship.

## Faith and mourning

Thomas Lynch, the poet, author and undertaker, says in his 1997 book, *The Undertaking: Life Studies from the Dismal Trade*, that at the time of death, a person is a "changeling." For family and friends, the person is "still there," and it is profoundly disrespectful to say that a body is "just a shell" in the early hours and days after a death. A funeral is a time when permission is given to mourners to say farewell to the mortal attributes and remains of someone who has died. In the Christian tradition, funerals are also a time to recognize that life does not end with death.

Because death can be a blow to the core beliefs we hold, a funeral seeks to gently remind people of those things that are sure and certain. In other words, a particular loss, however traumatic, does not mean that the whole structure of time and space has been suddenly dismantled. The gathering together of supportive people, the reciting of familiar words, and the actions of commending and committing someone to God help those who mourn to reconnect with life beyond their immediate loss. In this way a funeral brings saying farewell to an end, even as it provides a new foundation for those who mourn and a safe space to release the conflicted emotions of grief.

Balancing the needs of those who mourn, the wishes of those who have died, and the beliefs of the Church concerning death and funeral rites can be challenging. It is unfortunate when the content and tone of a funeral either ignore the reality of those who grieve or fail to name a greater reality than the person who has died.

In the Anglican tradition, funeral services are not the unique composition of the officiant. Authorized rites allow for flexibility within a basic structure and key prayers. These liturgies acknowledge grief in the light of glory, and offer rich words of consolation, comfort and hope. In this way, mourners are provided with a deeply reassuring atmosphere where grieving a loss, celebrating a life and commending an immortal soul to God can be accomplished.

# 6

# Does prayer make a difference?

Many soldiers on either side of battles pray to God before going into the fray. Some soldiers pray for victory, some for protection, some for peace of mind and steady nerves. Some of the soldiers who pray for victory get killed, and their side may lose the battle. Some who pray for protection may be wounded or captured. Some who pray for peace of mind end up traumatized.

Some Christians believe that faith in Jesus will result in success in this world – in athletics, business or family life, for example. Some even attribute their success to their faith in Jesus. I think that success has a lot more to do with hard work, acumen, or, in the case of athletes, genes.

Prayer is about uniting your soul with God. Christians believe that the Holy Spirit enables people to be drawn into the eternal prayer of Jesus, the Son, to God, the Father, the Creator of Creation. Praying is about freely sharing all the hopes, fears, cares, concerns and contradictions of your life with God, who loves you no matter what. Praying is about receiving love and forgiveness and strength to live in this world in a manner that is true to God.

In the life, death and resurrection of Jesus, God says that we are loved whether we win or lose, pass or fail – loved more than we love ourselves and loved more than anyone else can love us. Tuning into that love makes you a better person, and being a better person usually means being freer to love and serve other people. If that love makes someone run faster or achieve success of whatever kind, give glory to God!

## Praying for yourself

I pray for myself regularly and believe that such prayer is consistent with the Christian tradition.

The style of prayer that Jesus taught invites the faithful to acknowledge God as the transcendent Creator of all that is and all that will be. We are to ask God for the things we need to nurture and sustain us, the daily food that meets our physical and spiritual needs. We are to pray for grace to allow ourselves to see, forgive and amend our destructive ways, and to be equally forgiving of others. We are to pray that we will resist the temptation to say or do things that are harmful to the spirit, and that we will be given the strength and support to be drawn free from anything that would destroy the spirit. At the end of our prayer we ask for God's will to be the final guide for our lives.

My favourite personal prayer is attributed to St. Francis of Assisi: "Most high and glorious God, bring light to the darkness of my heart; give me right faith, certain hope, and perfect charity. Lord, give me insight and wisdom so I may always discern your holy and true will."

It is also important to pray for other people and situations; prayer is not about self-obsession. But in terms of becoming a more aware and effective agent of God's grace, regularly taking time to reflect on the rhythms of your journey, the good moments along with the bad, and always taking less time to speak and more time to listen deeply to the movement of God's Spirit will help you see possibilities for new ways of faithful living.

In the end, prayer for ourselves is part of drawing near to God, being in closer communion with God. The purpose of prayer is to unite our lives with God's profound goodness and to be filled with God's great desire to breathe hope and love, through us, into the world we all share.

## Does God always answer prayers?

I have a well-worn little book given to me as a boy called *In His Presence*. The book invites its readers to divide prayer time into four parts: adoration, confession, thanksgiving and supplication. You begin with adoring God. Think about the mystery and expanse of creation, of powerful love that knows no bounds, of the infinite and eternal God who comes to you in ways you can comprehend, giving you grace upon grace. Then, review your life (like playing back a tape of your day or week) and consider those things (done or undone) that have drawn you away from the love of God, gently confessing them to God, who has already forgiven you.

Review your life again, only this time consider those things that you are truly thankful for in your life, naming them also in prayer. Finally, offer to God all the cares and concerns of your heart, praying for others, for specific situations and for yourself. These prayers of supplication can be brief – a word or two, or a mental image. Concluding with a significant period of silent listening brings a well-balanced time of prayer to a close.

As you can see in this basic method, prayer is much more than asking for something and having God respond; prayer is primarily about attending to God even as you offer all the stuff of your life.

It is difficult to attend to God when you are full of yourself. Christians understand that God responds to all prayers with the Holy Spirit, who is our Comforter, Advocate and Guide. Specific prayers for specific things are fine to express, and if what you have prayed for comes to be, then be thankful; however, prayer is always answered by greater insight into the movement of God's Spirit. If your attention is fixed on whether you get what you ask for in prayer, you may be missing a good part of what you are being given.

## Fasting

In the Gospel of Matthew, Jesus has this to say about fasting: "Whenever you fast, do not look dismal like the hypocrites, for they disfigure their faces so as to show others that they are fasting. Truly I tell you, they have received their reward.

But when you fast put oil on your head and wash your face so that your fasting may be seen not by others but by your Father who is in secret; and your Father who sees in secret will reward you."

These words are often read in churches on Ash Wednesday, which begins the season of Lent, a time of penitence and pardon. Along with Good Friday, Ash Wednesday is one of two major "fast days" in the Christian tradition.

Fasting essentially involves going without food. A fast may be observed in varying degrees, ranging from forgoing a meal to doing without food for several days (never more than 72 hours, and always with some water). Sometimes longer fasts include partaking in a meagre meal or "collation" each day.

Fasting is different from abstinence, which entails going without certain kinds of food or other activities. Most people are familiar with the practice of abstinence during the forty days of Lent. Sometimes Christians practise abstinence on Fridays, the day of the week when Jesus was crucified.

While it is easy to describe fasting as the mechanical exercise of avoiding food, this does little to describe the nature of a religious fast. The practice actually has very little to do with what is given up. Fasting is not about dieting or serving some kind of bodily need, nor is it about punishing the body or making a political statement – although going hungry to stand in solidarity with others or to draw attention to some cause can speak volumes.

Instead, fasting is a conscious and self-disciplined attempt to create tangible space in one's life for the Creator of Creation. It is an act of prayerful devotion or a way of expressing hunger for God. Fasting, like abstinence, involves intentionally doing something different from an ordinary or expected routine, so that as we miss what we have given up, we are reminded of who is being honoured and whose will is being sought.

Fasting may be described as "praying with the whole body." It is important to stress, however, that fasting is not about jeopardizing bodily health – or, for that matter, doing anything that draws a lot of attention to ourselves. Ideally, fasting is a quiet, prayerful gesture observed on special days in the Christian calendar, or for special reasons in our personal journey.

## Get rich quick?

Not too long ago, much publicity surrounded a book containing a prayer that was said to lead to personal wealth. I think that publishing a certain class of self-help book is probably a more likely way to get rich! As for finding prayers or religious advice to help us along the path of life, the Lord's Prayer is very well balanced and applicable to most needs, desires or temptations people may face.

Some people erroneously equate earthly prosperity with piety or righteous living. Some Christians believe that God will make great material gains happen if you believe the right things, pray for the right things and act in the right ways. This type of thinking is a bit difficult to accept for the rest of us, who find that solid faith doesn't necessarily lead to economic gain, good health and a life of ease.

Jesus had a fair bit to say about wealth, usually in the context of telling people that their treasure shall be where their heart is. He spoke of the importance of seeking the riches of God: eternal, spiritual riches. Primarily, he encouraged people to love one another in a manner that reflected the nature of God. His followers understood this, and one of them, Paul of Tarsus, wrote that to live by the Spirit of God means striving for love, joy, peace, patience, kindness, generosity, faithfulness, gentleness and self-control. Paul said that if we live by the Spirit, let us also walk by the Spirit.

I believe that God wants peace, wholeness and happiness for each person, and that God's will is for each person to enable this to happen for others. The Christian message is concerned with making people aware that God is present to each person, regardless of material or physical well-being, and that following God has absolutely nothing to do with self-aggrandizement.

## The Lord's Prayer

At the heart of Christian prayer is the prayer of Jesus, known as the Lord's Prayer. The Lord's Prayer has two basic parts: three petitions glorify God, and three concern human needs (for sustenance, for forgiveness and for help in times of trial).

An integral part of this prayer is a recognition of the primacy of God's will. Praying oneself into the will of God becomes even more significant as Christians reflect on Jesus kneeling under the ancient olive trees in the early hours of Good Friday in the Garden of Gethsemane, overlooking the dark Kidron Valley and the walls of Jerusalem above it. Jesus falls on his face and prays, "My Father, if it is possible, let this cup pass from me; yet not what I want but what you want."

It may well be that the only worthwhile prayer is that which draws us into a closer understanding of the movement and development of God's will. To pray in this way is to place your own particular concerns in the context of a much more intricate and expansive whole, where who you are and what you seek can only be fully grasped when the wider sweep of God's hand is felt.

If you see prayer as leading to the possibility of divine favours, such as getting a break every now and then, or having a specific type of help in a particular situation, then prayer may seem like playing a slot machine. If, instead, your prayer seeks to draw you more fully into an awareness and understanding of the course of God's will, you may find that prayer is like attending to a rich polyphony, where the particular strain of music that you need to hear will sound clearly to you as you become more familiar with the many layers of music that speak of God's creative purpose.

# 7

# What role does the Bible play?

The Christian Bible contains the "Canon of Holy Scriptures," or the list of books that have been certified by the Church as dependable channels of the Word of God. Using myth, poetry, history, prophecy and proclamation, the Bible reveals God through human language and experience.

There are dozens of transparently sacred moments in the Bible, timeless words that speak of God's powerful and demanding love or of the plaintive prayers of women and men. Psalm 139 is a poignant example of divine love and human response.

Many other moments are clearly not very holy, and say more about particular people in specific social situations. St. Paul's wish for those who are upsetting his flock in Galatians 5:12 is a noteworthy example of purely human expression.

The Bible tells the story of God and what God does. It tells of creation and redemption, and reveals the strong foundations of human faith in a God who lovingly enters into human lives to offer hope. The Bible is the Word of God in the words of people. An astute mind can easily see the difference and be delighted and inspired.

## Different versions of the Bible

Each part of the Bible was written within a specific set of historical circumstances by people who spoke either Hebrew or Greek. As Christianity spread, the Bible was translated into a wider range of languages (often against the wishes of those who felt that the Latin Bible should be the only authoritative text). English versions of the Bible were in existence long before the well-known King James Bible was published in 1611. There are now more than 2,000 different translations of the Bible.

Contemporary English versions of the Bible translate Greek and Hebrew texts in either a literal or "dynamic" manner. This means that versions will be more or less similar to one another depending on the style of translation that is used. It also means that versions can range from very loose and sometimes slanted paraphrases to highly accurate renderings of original texts into English.

In the Anglican Church, the Bible is central and essential, but it is not the sole authority. Scripture, tradition and reason are closely intertwined, such that the Church is guided by the constant interplay of the Word of God, the accumulated wisdom and practice of the Church, and the discerning minds of each new generation of Christians. For this reason, caution is exercised in the choice of Bible used for worship and study, and the preference is for accurate translations of the original Greek and Hebrew texts.

## Prophets

The best way to tell whether a prophet has knowledge of the future is to wait around and see what happens. If events unfold the way a prophet "predicts," then you could say that the future had been "foretold." This is not unlike listening to polls: if events happen the way the polls predicted, then you'd say, "Good pollster!" If something different than predicted happens, you'd say, "Polls are useless. I don't know why people even bother with them."

We understand a prophet to be one who speaks on behalf of God. In the ancient Nicene Creed of the Christian Church, we state that the Holy Spirit has "spoken through the prophets," revealing the progression of God's great desire to reveal God's love, through the Messiah, to all the world – and to have this love received. The prophet is one who delivers messages from God to other people – messages that declare God's will and call people to respond to it as soon as possible. This is very different from being clairvoyant or being able to predict the future.

Scripture scholar Walter Vogels, in a book called *The Prophet, a Man of God: The Interior Life of the Prophet* (1982), takes a very different approach to understanding the prophet. Vogels is less concerned with the content of a prophet's message than with the relationship he has with God, and how that relationship compelled the prophet to speak and act in certain ways towards the people of his time. It becomes very clear that the principal concern of prophets is to tell what God has told them to tell, for the benefit of the specific people God has sent them to meet.

In other words, a prophet seeks to express or tell forth the mind of God rather than to foretell the future. The prophet is not concerned with giving accurate details of historical events, but with drawing people to recognize and receive the unfolding of God's purpose in the midst of historical events.

## The biblical view of women

If a culture favours the role of men, then its history, including its experience of God, will be recorded through the eyes of men. If those who interpret history are influenced by a patriarchal culture, then the understanding of history will favour a male perspective, and will reinforce whatever gender biases may exist.

The Bible tells the story of God's love through the imperfect lens of human culture. This means that the prevailing cultural norms that gave men predominance in the time of Abraham, Moses and Jesus affect the tone of the Bible, just as the interpretation of the Bible over the years has been influenced by similar norms. Although the Bible affirms that women and men are equal before God and that God's love is freely extended to all people, culture often acts to subvert the word of God.

Even though much of the Bible and its interpretation have been affected by cultures dominated by men, people of both sexes have always been able to receive, understand and rejoice in its central message of redeeming and empowering love. This is because God transcends culture and lovingly enters into the lives of women, men and children in equal measure. It is probably no accident that the Risen Christ first appeared to women – a fact attested by the gospels of Matthew, Mark, Luke and John. This striking placement of women in the very dawning of the Christian faith does much to bring a female perspective into the unfolding story of God's love for all.

## Creation and the environment

Many people single out chapter 1 of Genesis as proof that God and God's adherents hold an ideological position that has caused the destruction of the environment. If you read the whole chapter, however, it is clear that men and women are to tend the earth because it is the source of food. This idea is also present in the second creation story, in chapter 2, where humanity is depicted as being woven into nature as caretaker. The biblical notion that the earth must be "subdued" for our "dominion" is less a call to conquer at all costs than a call to find accommodation in the impersonal and often harsh forces of nature.

The distortion of the created order by human activity is nevertheless a common theme in the Bible.

The story of Adam and Eve describes the human desire to grasp beyond what is patently good. The myth tells us that in this grasping, humanity loses awareness of itself as part of the created order, and overemphasizes itself as a creator of order, an imperfect shaper of its own world. Sadly, the desire for more takes humanity farther from what has already been given, and it becomes estranged from its own true nature. In the end humanity feels alone, sitting in the mess it has made of things.

A 1997 report called *Toward Sustainable Community*, prepared by the Task Force on Churches and Corporate Responsibility, states that "God has created the whole cosmos to be good…a common inheritance for all peoples for all times." It says that in a just and moral economy, the whole created order is treated with utmost respect and reverence rather than exploited and degraded; people are enabled to participate fully in decisions that affect their lives; and public and private interests are accountable and held responsible for the social and environmental impacts of their operations.

To accuse traditional monotheistic religions of being a major cause of environmental degradation requires heroic oversimplification. It is much more astute to look to industry, agriculture, multinational corporations or anyone who runs sewage directly into rivers to find the major causes of ecological damage. Religion may be more accurately seen as part of the solution.

# 8

# Is there any sense to all the confusion?

The number and extent of issues that are presenting themselves at the dawn of the twenty-first century are staggering. We are connected to a vast flow of information that readily abounds on nearly every subject, and the world seems to be changing all too quickly. How nice it would be to have our faith bolstered by constant affirmations, encouragement and support, in schools, the marketplace and the workplace, by the media and in the corridors of power. Instead, there seem to be walls dividing society and the sacred, as if there is no common ground between the two.

Gaining perspective means looking at issues in systematic and specific ways, rather than being overwhelmed with everything at once; thinking critically about what is being presented; and trying to bring "faithful" thoughts into the conversation. Sometimes your faithful thoughts may be the only ones that make sense. At other times, the interplay of what you are seeing and feeling with what you believe may produce a different perspective altogether.

## Pornography

An outrage-provoking scandal involving the condemnation and dismissal of a high-ranking military officer who had downloaded pornography onto his work computer brings to mind a story in John's gospel. Some people brought before Jesus a woman who had committed adultery and therefore would be executed. To the captors he said, "Let those of you without sin cast the first stone." Soon, Jesus and the woman were the only ones remaining. He then said to her, "Where are they who would condemn you? Neither do I condemn you. Go your way, and sin no more." A poignant moral tale for anyone who would condemn or be condemned.

It is reasonable to say that those who hold certain offices are obliged to observe the standards set by their organizations, and must be prepared to face the consequences of inappropriate actions. At the same time, organizations that place heavy responsibilities on individuals ought to ensure that proper supports are in place for the mere mortals who hold such offices. People who work under public scrutiny in stressful conditions can become prone to seeking out distractions that are unhealthy. Leaders are fallible human beings.

The abundance of pornography on the Internet exists because lots of people want it to be there, evidently for purposes of exhibition, gratification or monetary gain. Pornography is an exploitation of other human beings and a distortion of healthy sexuality and human relationships. It is not a creative, life-giving or life-affirming enterprise, and the world would be much better off without it. The reality is that individuals can choose to make or view pornography, both within or outside the law, and healthy consciences are probably the only deterrents to its proliferation.

## Gambling

Several dioceses of the Anglican Church have passed motions stating that the continued and expanding use of lotteries and other games of chance to fund the programs of governments and other public institutions is deplorable. These motions also urged other churches to actively discourage the practice of all games of chance and raffles as a means of raising money. Finally, they encourage and support equitable systems and policies of taxation in the public sector, and a "lively and comprehensive understanding of Christian stewardship" for all members of the Church.

Gambling is a multi-billion-dollar industry in Canada that generates huge revenues for governments, charities and other groups or individuals. The allure of revenues for the organizers of lotteries, charitable gaming, video lottery terminals or horse racing, and the funding that this often provides for charitable works or other services, has created a situation where gambling appears to have become, somewhat perversely, an integral part of our society.

It is against this very pragmatic backdrop that many questions and concerns about the well-being of our society, of families and of individuals emerge. The real and present reality of problem gambling and the belief that gambling revenues represent a regressive form of taxation have raised a steady voice of protest.

The protest against gambling is often received as a wet blanket on a wonderful party where goodwill, fun and enticing possibilities are being celebrated. It takes courage and conviction to make such a protest, and individuals or organizations making the protest must review their own fundraising activities and modify them accordingly.

## Murder and grief

Too many people around the world suffer the violent and traumatic loss of loved ones, and become unwitting objects of public scrutiny. When this type of loss happens to us or to someone close to us, we know (or we quickly learn) how to behave and what to do at a funeral; what is less clear is how to be and what to do in the weeks that follow. Those most affected by loss must be patient with themselves and others as everybody seeks to come to terms with what has happened, each in his or her own way.

It is normal for people to experience a range of sometimes overwhelming emotions in the months after suffering sudden, violent loss. It is important to attend to the movements of grief, allowing time to sift the jumble of thoughts, prayers and practicalities. Having others around who can listen, support, comfort or counsel can be helpful – not just in the early days, but also during the longer time it can take to discover all the ways life has changed and to rediscover meaning, purpose and hope.

For those who seek to help, thoughtful gestures and knowing when to give space can be just as important as words, particularly when there is nothing obvious to say. Simply listening with compassion and understanding can be a great gift. Inviting people to do ordinary things can be a refreshing break from intense expressions of concern – especially for children. Everyone will need to let the exceptional slowly be replaced by the everyday.

At the same time, it cannot be denied that the tragedy has deeply affected the families and friends of victims – and, in many cases, those of a perpetrator. The community as a whole is affected also, reminding everyone of how fragile human life is and how carefully we must treasure all those we are given by God to love.

## Tolerance and acceptance

Many of the things that disturb our sense of peace are hard to understand: racism, armed conflict, the crippling debt of the world's poorest countries, ecological degradation and homelessness are a few of the many reminders that we live out our lives against a backdrop of unsettling situations. Perhaps being disturbed by these things can be a first step in seeking meaningful ways to respond to them. Perhaps the best response is to teach our children that there is a better way of living.

The seventeenth-century philosopher John Locke, writing in a time of religious intolerance, said that toleration is "the chief characteristic mark of the true church." Tolerance is an important virtue, and we need to teach our children how to recognize bigotry or prejudice. However, children also need to know that there are limits to tolerance.

Sometimes people confuse tolerance with simply "putting up" with something or someone, or think that it is somehow improper to question other people's beliefs or actions. Children need to be aware that the behaviour or views of others can be questioned – and be accepted, rejected or resisted.

It is not intolerant to carefully and respectfully consider another person's beliefs, causes or opinions, and then decide whether they are worthy of acceptance. I believe tolerance is a conscious attitude we reach when we take the time to understand the positions of others and decide to accept differences without acrimony or prejudice.

Jesus' commandment to "love one another" has very little to do with just putting up with everybody or everything. To love means to seriously engage people. It means seeking truth, accepting and celebrating those things that affirm life, and questioning those things that appear to harm life.

The Letter to the Hebrews describes the word of God as "living and active," sharply discerning "the thoughts and intentions of the heart." Tolerance is born from a desire to love in an open and discerning manner.

## Public execution

When I visited Oklahoma City in April 2001, I was struck by the candour and courage of those who had rallied together following the horrific 1995 bombing and had constructed a poignant national memorial on the site of that act of terrorism. The purpose of the memorial is to "remember those who were killed, those who survived, and those changed forever." Most importantly, it is meant to help all who visit to know the impact of violence, and to "offer comfort, strength, peace, hope, and serenity."

Traumatic loss of any description attacks the spirit, leaching out our sense of safety, trust, value and control, and often alienating us from others. The Oklahoma City Memorial does not dwell on the trauma caused by the choices made by Timothy McVeigh; instead, it enables people to find hope and restoration by creating a tranquil and safe haven in a place where violence once ruled. I sensed that the anticipation and attention surrounding McVeigh's execution, scheduled for May 2001, disturbed that hard-won tranquility.

The broadcast of the execution fulfilled the law of the State of Oklahoma and rewarded those who are drawn to the idea of seeing someone being killed. It cannot restore normalcy to those who lost a loved one, or bring peace to those with horrific memories. If McVeigh had been killed just before he detonated the bomb, then his death would have saved many innocent lives; to kill him after the fact, and to broadcast it to a world that needs relief from violence, is devoid of good purpose.

A statue beside the site of the bombing depicts Jesus weeping at such senseless carnage. Perhaps he wept again in May 2001 when the cameras rolled and a profoundly misguided young man died.

## Church apologies

Each situation involving a church's apology for historical misdeeds is different and needs to be assessed on its own merits. Nevertheless, it is possible to address in a general way the issue of whether saying sorry is enough by considering what may motivate such an apology.

Perhaps one of the best ways of testing the motive behind an apology is to consider whether the one apologizing seeks something in return. If the apology of a church, or any other body, is politically motivated and is used to force an expression of forgiveness – or some other kind of settlement – then one may well ask whether saying sorry is enough.

In the Christian tradition, the idea of contrition is used to describe the motivation for confession. Contrition involves profound sorrow and disdain for some action or omission. Contrition occurs when the grace of God allows a person (or a church) to see his or her life in the revealing and sometimes disconcerting light of Christ. As particular actions, omissions or attitudes become transparent as barriers to fullness of life, it becomes intolerable not to confess them.

Although contrition may motivate confession, it is repentance – a willingness to actually change or make amends – that provides the concrete sign of genuine confession. Offering an apology to those who have been wronged can be an indicator of repentance. However, in the absence of other concrete changes in behaviour or attitudes, one might be inclined to test the sincerity of any apology. I would hope that Christian churches are motivated by grace to offer apologies for past misdeeds and are also conspicuously repentant.

The other side of contrition and repentance is forgiveness. A contrite confession, apology and actual repentance can create for all concerned an opportunity for new possibilities. An aggrieved party may be enabled to forgive and get on with life, relinquishing feelings of anxiety, anger, hurt or pain. A repentant party may be similarly liberated when forgiveness is offered, no longer feeling bound or burdened by concealment, guilt or shame.

God's forgiveness is already present when there is contrition and repentance, and this can be made outward and visible to someone in the sacrament of reconciliation. Forgiveness may or may not be forthcoming from an aggrieved individual or group, however, and those who apologize, even with the purest motives, may simply have to accept this and try to move on.

## Health care

When a person is ill the world becomes very small, often limited to the place of pain and uncertainty. Dependence upon others for care affects one's sense of dignity, and often the manifestations of illness affect feelings of worth or attractiveness. Depression, anxiety, apathy and even grieving the loss of health are other shadows in the world of one who is ill. Grave illness can add a layer of spiritual insecurity when people probe for meaning as they face their own mortality.

It is disconcerting when universal health care is deemed to be expendable or is compromised by limited funding. While private health-care facilities can easily govern case loads and find a profitable balance between revenues and expenditures, they are an attractive alternative only for those who can afford the option. Giving to hospital charities is noble, but relying on individuals to augment insufficient hospital funding (often by lotteries, it seems) is a regressive form of taxation.

In my experience as a pastor and as a patient, I have seen health-care professionals precariously balance large case loads against patients who expect timely and thorough responses to their concerns. Waiting with uncertainty appears to be the common experience of patients; dividing attention and limited resources equitably and in a timely way appears to be the common experience of physicians, nurses and technicians.

Health care operates in the context of real, often vivid, human experiences of need. The kind and quality of health services provided can dramatically affect the process of restoring health or of maintaining quality of life when chronic or palliative care is required. Ideally, our public health-care system is primarily concerned with extending skill, compassion and comfort to people who are vulnerable, no matter what their social standing. Rationalizing hospital services, eliminating redundancy, and watching the bottom line are obviously necessary; it is also necessary to think attentively about the particular experiences of those who are injured, ill or dying. Generous measures should be taken by our governments to provide for those who give and receive such care.

## Astrology and horoscopes

Astrology purports that the stars influence human history and that a person's fortunes can be forecast from the position of the stars at the moment of birth. The presence of daily horoscopes in most newspapers and the abundance of such literature at checkout counters suggest that astrology holds much fascination for people today.

Astrology falls under the more general category of divination, which is the "skill" of predicting future events, often by occult, or supernatural, means. Other forms of divination include reading palms, studying the entrails of sacrificial animals, interpreting omens or signs, and communicating with the dead.

Although the word "astrology" appears only once or twice in the Bible, the more general practice of divination receives much negative attention, including its strict prohibition in the books of Leviticus and Deuteronomy. Biblical condemnation of divination likens it to idolatry, or the worship of a human creation that is held to have the powers of God, often for the rather self-serving purpose of trying to place oneself in as favourable a position as possible.

Astrology is not a practice of the Christian tradition, and it is therefore not possible for the Church to either recommend or condone the practice of checking horoscopes. At best, astrology innocuously fascinates people; at worst, it is a vain attempt to grasp at knowledge that is simply not accessible to anyone. The future is God's, and human fortunes are better influenced by holier pursuits.

# Holiday time

The trend to refer to everything that happens between mid-December and early January as the "holiday season" is for some people appalling, for some laughable and for others inevitable. This term doesn't bother me, because the annual phenomenon it denotes has very little to do with the four weeks of Advent that precede Christmas Day, with Christmastide, or with the Feast of Stephen (the first Christian martyr) on December 26, not to mention the twelve days of Christmas (like the song) that concludes with the day of Epiphany (January 6).

The reds and greens, the ubiquitous music and the prompting to spend that occur from October to December pale in contrast to the vibrant blue of Advent, when the comforting words of Isaiah and the discomfiting challenges of John the Baptist give substantial food for thought – such as turning from individual behaviours that are destructive or pondering how God will complete creation at the end of all time.

If some want to lobby school boards, shopping malls or government officials to make Christmas reappear in the vernacular of Canadian society, so be it. In the meantime, I hope everybody who really cares about preserving the integrity of this Christian holy day will keep things simple and resist the temptation to give – all at once – every good gift, kind act or nice thought. Better to let the "holiday season's" confusing overtones and complex undertones run their own course.

## Same-sex marriage

In Canada we are privileged to have freedom of speech. This means that a person can express religious beliefs, without fear, in public debate. The same right extends to people who are concerned about examining issues outside of the matrix of religious belief.

In the case of legalizing same-sex marriage, lawmakers were compelled to consider whether the rights, responsibilities, freedoms and limitations afforded to a man and a woman who seek to marry could be extended to include any two persons who seek to marry.

The primary framework for public debate on this issue has been defined by principles of law and notions of equality. A secondary and determining factor is whether trends in Canadian society (which include all varieties of religious and non-religious belief) have moved things into a place where a change in the legal definition of marriage is possible and practicable.

For some organized religious bodies in Canada, the possibility for debate on same-sex marriage is simply untenable. For others, there is due process to allow for discernment and decision within a framework that considers religious beliefs and values. Regardless of how a decision is reached, religious bodies have the right to determine who is eligible to participate in their marriage rituals.

We live in a democracy; so many different religions and denominations can peacefully coexist because we have laws that prohibit the legislating of belief. Religious belief can and ought to be expressed, but it is not the determining factor in public debate on this type of issue. Lawmakers must look with great care to principles that will ensure a balance between freedom, social cohesion and equality. Religious bodies must respect the fact that these same principles allow them the right to abide by the tenets of their beliefs.

## Designing babies

From time to time we hear stories of couples who wish to have some control over the genetic makeup of their child before it is conceived. For example, a few years ago two deaf lesbians wanted to optimize by medical intervention their likelihood of having a deaf baby.

The question of tailoring offspring to suit the desires of parents presents much difficulty. If children can be conceived in the hope that they have the attribute of deafness, so can they be conceived with the intention of their being taller, prettier or smarter. This practice opens the door to the possibility of aborting fetuses with "undesirable" attributes, and the slippery slope of "customizing" children.

In the best of all worlds, children are conceived in love and, no matter what abilities or disabilities they are born with, are received into a family and community that will affirm them, provide for them, and enable them to grow into people with lives that are as whole and rich as possible. This calls forth commitment and compassion from all of us; these are positive, constructive and life-giving responses, and it is good for people to see them as essential to our nature as individuals and as a community.

I believe that the conception of life is sacred, and that the intention of parents who choose to bear children ought to be philosophical, allowing nature to run its course, and knowing that parenting of whatever order will ask much of them. In the end, leaving the designer element to those who make baby clothes is a more faithful way to proceed.

## Organ donations

The Multiple Organ Retrieval and Exchange (MORE) Program of Ontario has published an excellent document entitled *Pastoral Guide to Organ and Tissue Donation*. This booklet suggests that fewer than half of those who say they are willing to donate organs have actually signed a donor card. Their research suggests that one of the barriers to signing a donor card is an assumption that there are religious constraints to organ donation.

The MORE booklet concludes, "In fact, the opposite is true. All major religions do support organ donations. The beliefs may differ slightly from denomination to denomination, but the underlying theme is always the same: Organ and tissue donation represents the principles on which all religions are based – loving, caring and giving." People who have questions about organ donation may wish to have a discussion with a member of their clergy to see whether any particular conditions apply.

As a Christian, I see organ donation as an act of altruistic love, patterned on the example of Jesus, who gave his life that we may have life in its fullness.

I first signed a donor card many years ago. I did so with complete confidence in the resurrection faith, which is at the heart of all I believe. Although our human bodies will eventually die, we continue to be distinct persons, created and loved by God. The words of Paul's First Letter to the Corinthians are compelling: "Listen, I will tell you a mystery! We will not all die, but we will all be changed, in a moment, in the twinkling of an eye, at the last trumpet."

In the face of such glorious promise and hope for our immortal souls, the act of leaving our mortal body to the service of others is easy to contemplate. Signing a donor card (and telling others you have done so) is a good way to make sure this actually happens.

## Conditional organ donations

A group of parents in Ontario wanted to donate their kidneys in order to free up funds to pay for their special needs' children's education after funding was cut back. In Pennsylvania, there has been some discussion of paying relatives of posthumous donors. Are these morally acceptable practices?

These two cases are different in appearance but similar in nature. One appears to involve people offering to donate their kidneys as a way of making a dramatic political statement about government education policies concerning children with special needs. The other involves the state creating an incentive to encourage posthumous organ donation and increase the supply of organs for needy recipients.

At best, these two situations are morally neutral. Both seek to enable the well-being of others, but both also make organ donation conditional upon an outcome that benefits the donor or donor's family. This opens up a very disturbing and morally unacceptable scenario.

If organ donation becomes tied to any kind of economic or political gain, organs become commodities. If organs become commodities, then organ "donation" becomes a matter of who needs money and who can afford to pay – a situation that would almost certainly favour the wealthy over the needy.

All major religions support organ and tissue donation as an act of loving, caring and giving. Being a donor is a way of giving that does not create the obligation of exchange between the donor and the recipient. It is an act of freely giving to another. For Christians, this act is patterned on the example of Jesus.

If every person of every faith that supports and encourages organ and tissue donation grasped this idea and acted upon it, it is likely that the number of donations would easily meet the need and remove the danger of turning human body parts into commodities that can be bought, sold or bartered.

## Stem-cell research

On September 11, 2001, at 8:00 a.m., a media release from Washington announced that a panel of experts from the National Academy of Sciences strongly endorsed human embryonic stem-cell research and stated that government-funded research is the best way to achieve promising medical breakthroughs. A couple of hours later, the media was transfixed by the horrific violation of human life as terrorists flew planes into buildings in Washington and New York.

In a perfect world, human minds are given over to the care and well-being of each other, and technology operates to improve the quality of life for all people and for the planet we share. The reality is that the human propensity to pursue extremes is an ever-present slippery slope. If a commercial aircraft can become a missile, the procedures and products of stem-cell research can also be employed to adversely affect the common good.

While a perverse distortion of aviation technology does not mean we must stop using aircraft, we need to take stringent measures to ensure that human life is not placed at risk. In the same way, the possibility that stem-cell research may perversely lead some towards the commodification of embryos or genetic customizing does not mean we must condemn the entire enterprise; however, clear and enforceable regulations must be in place.

The Canadian Institute of Health Research in recent years reviewed a number of recommendations concerning stem-cell research as it continues to develop regulations for the Government of Canada. These recommendations appear to be heading in the direction of being sensible and respectful of the sanctity of human life.

I believe that God invites us to share in the work of creation in ways that are life-giving, and that there is often a very fine line dividing good from evil in how the products of human intelligence and technology are employed. The spectre of malevolence should never be allowed to stop the promise of hope; if it did, we would become immobilized. However, it is obvious that vigilance must always accompany any kind of human endeavour.

## Medical technologies

Generally speaking, the development of new medical technologies, such as artificial hearts, is religiously neutral. These procedures seek to enable the well-being of others, and are a good example of how humans can work to alleviate suffering and benefit the common good. This is God's will for human ingenuity.

Several years ago I benefited from sophisticated surgery that cured me of ulcerative colitis; before that surgery I took expensive medications to control the disease. I am often struck by the fact that people in other parts of the world continue to suffer and probably die from the same disease because information, medicine and surgical skills are not available to them.

It is important to ask how people throughout the world will be able to benefit from the development of new medical technologies. Do these have a greater medical priority than, say, the development of a treatment or vaccine for AIDS, especially given its epidemic spread in the southern hemisphere, or the eradication of common infectious diseases, such as tuberculosis or measles, which continue to afflict many people in developing countries?

Medical technology should always be exposed to probing scrutiny, in terms of both considering the sanctity of human life and asking how the benefits of new ways of healing will be extended to as many people as possible. True religion results in a spirit of altruism. If the many wonderful developments of medicine serve only affluent people and countries, then there is every reason for people of faith to pause, look to the essential nature of religious belief, and strive to ensure that the most needy are also served.

## Animal organs in humans

In considering whether it is ethically acceptable to transplant animal organs or tissues into humans, it is helpful to approach the question in different ways. One way is to compare the use of animals for food with the use of animals for medicine. Most people do not consider it wrong to raise animals for nutrition, or to use the byproducts of meat production for fertilizer, clothing or other benefits to people. It is not too difficult to step from the accepted practice of using parts of animals for human food to using parts of animals for human medicine.

If we accept that it is ethically acceptable to use animals for human benefit, then we must consider how such animals are bred and raised. We have laws that protect animals from cruel treatment; if animals used for medical purposes are treated in the same humane manner as animals raised for food, this would reinforce the idea that there is little difference between using animals for either purpose.

What begins to complicate things, however, is the practice of genetically altering or enhancing animals for a particular purpose. Food production is concerned with maximizing volume with minimum time and cost. Hence, the breeding of bigger or more productive animals happens frequently, and some animals begin to take on characteristics that would not otherwise have come about.

If we apply the same methods to breeding animals for human medicine, and if we introduce the idea of genetically altering animals to be more "human-like" in order to produce a superior supply of organs for medical transplants, then a very dubious situation arises. The prospect of breeding some new kind of "spare parts" creature begs the question of how far we can or should go before we fundamentally violate the integrity of creation.

Questions about what may or may not be ethically acceptable involve carefully considering issues from many different angles – there is no religious rule book that gives all the answers. Ethically acceptable solutions emerge when people are willing to articulate and respect boundaries. Within certain boundaries it may be ethically acceptable to use animal organs in people: without or beyond certain boundaries it may not be.

## The end of the world

In Book Eleven of St. Augustine's *Confessions*, he notes that the past is no more, the future is not yet, and the present must immediately become the past, because if it didn't, it would be eternity instead of time. His argument that time may not actually exist probably won't prevent some people from seizing any opportunity to say what God may have in mind as our human clocks and calendars mark the passing of another thousand years.

I think that Jesus' best advice on this subject can be found in Matthew 24:36 – No one knows except God. The prudent teaching of Jesus is to be ready to meet God face to face at any moment. Being ready has a lot to do with loving God and all that God has made; it has little to do with the passing or beginning of a millennium.

For Christians, Holy Week is an occasion of remembering Jesus' passionate journey – in the same human time we journey by – to the cross. It is a time of remembering God's steadfast faithfulness, forgiveness and everlasting love in the face of our human weaknesses, and our frequent complicity in denying and destroying what God has made in favour of our own creations.

On Thursday in Holy Week, Christians gather together to remember the Last Supper, when Jesus said that bread, a simple food, and wine, a common drink, would become his very life, a sign of God's close companionship with us on earth and an offering of reconciliation and spiritual food. We remember that Jesus was taken from his disciples, leaving them and generations to come with the words and actions that still make him present in the narrow confines of time.

On Good Friday we gather to remember Jesus' suffering and death on a cross. We also bring to mind all the pain, suffering, evil and sorrow in the world. But it is Good or God's Friday because in allowing Jesus' horrible execution and in Jesus' refusal to deny who he was, God revealed that God is with us in every aspect of life. Not even the darkest moments of our lives, the worst things we do to others or the greatest burdens we bear can separate us from the strong, saving hands of God.

Our experience of time, and all the joys and sorrows that we encounter as finite beings, is made meaningful by these glimpses of eternity. God creates us to freely choose what we will embrace in life, but does not abandon us to the whims of human will or the impartial flow of nature. For those who can grasp this gift and share the love behind it, there is every reason to look to the future with hope.

# Conclusion

Good questions lead to more questions, and the quest for answers keeps us engaged with life and the Creator. A good answer is one that stands apart, less a personal statement than something objective that speaks both to the one who provided it and those who hear it. In the end, truth is not the property of any individual, and as life spins each of us around, it is possible to encounter, as a questioner, the words we once provided as an answer.

Many of the responses in this book are compass points that give just enough bearing to venture more deeply into the question, issue or experience, or to realize that a change of course is in order. In either case, it can be satisfying to get to a place where we can make such a decision in the soft light of wisdom that pierces the darkness.

As you quest beyond these words, you may discover that some of them have become your own, others may have been discarded, and still others linger for you to ponder further – or will return when your journey brings them to you again. Perhaps you will discover entirely new ways of seeing the same things. As long as you hold to the way ahead, the possibilities are endless.

May the winds of God refresh, strengthen, uphold and challenge you on your way.